365 brilliant ideas
for getting off your
backside and living
life to the full

be
arsed

First published in 2009 by
The Infinite Ideas Company Limited
36 St Giles
Oxford, OX1 3LD
United Kingdom
www.infideas.com

infinite ideas

A CIP catalogue record for this book is available from the British Library

ISBN 978-1-905940-94-3

Cover and text designed by Cylinder

Typeset by Cylinder

Printed in China

Start here, start now

The book entitled *Don't Be Arsed*, if someone could be bothered to write it, would be a major work of literature. If you really can't be fagged, blessed are you to be born at this time. Thanks to the wonders of science eight decades of comfortably not doing very much literally yawns ahead of you.

For the twenty-first century couch potato there is a truly thrilling array of ways not to be bothered. Sofas have never been comfier or more affordable. Beds have never been more relaxing. The exciting work of food scientists in the last 10 years has bequeathed to the nation a golden age of fancy biscuits which, thanks to the crusading innovative zeal of supermarkets, are delivered to within centimetres of our open mouths.

Ask your parents about the dark ages before satellite television when there were only three channels and one of them didn't broadcast during the afternoon. The horror! And don't forget in those days people didn't have TV remote controls. Ordinary people – sometimes children as young as eight – were forced to walk across an entire room to change the channel several times every evening. Nowadays we have the privilege of flicking channels without having to interrupt our gentle drooling and dozing.

Thanks to the god of indolence, those of you who've been a bit knackered for the last twenty years can now lie virtually motionless for many weeks at a time – provided you have a pizza delivery menu within arm's reach and a strong bladder. What's the point, you may ask, in messing things up by trying to do something different? "Trying," as the most distinguished contemporary philosopher of can't-be-arsedness* tells us, "is the first step towards failure."

So stick this book in the loo where it can't do any harm, crack open a beer, microwave some popcorn, put the snooker on, maybe have a snooze, and… WAKE UP! WHAT ARE YOU THINKING? This can't-be-arsed thing has gone on long enough. One day you are going to realise that you're not just boring other people, you're even boring yourself.

You might have reached that stage already, and you're furtively reading this introduction in the bookshop, wondering if it's too late or too difficult to stir yourself. It's not. We're not promising you will lose 10lb in a week, become irresistible to the opposite sex, or suddenly be fabulously rich overnight. Instead we offer ideas that will make your life a bit more fun and make you a bit more successful and a bit happier. All you have to do is to be stimulated enough to try them out.

* Homer Simpson, of course

We've heard all your excuses. You don't have the time? Lots of these ideas take five minutes or less. You don't have the cash? Most of them are free. You're worried you will look silly? What do you think you look like when you're snoring in an armchair with the remains of a kebab on your gut?

Be honest, the only real excuse is that you can't be arsed.

Often self-help books end up by making you hate yourself. If you don't have the job of your dreams or a washboard stomach by the time you reach page 190 you feel like a failure, and resolve not to try anything like that again. But in the real world there's no shame in small failures from time to time, just as long as you keep wanting to try something else new. "What is this 'something'?" you ask, "I'm fresh out of ideas." This is where we come in. Our experts, who are pretty experienced at being arsed, have contributed 365 of them for you. These ideas have little risk and in a small way might change your life for the better. And here's an extra tip: they work better if you switch off the snooker first.

Infinite Ideas

be arsed...
to get your
body going

(no, pint lifting doesn't count as exercise)

1

1

Have a direct debit for your gym membership, and go! Someone with well-toned muscles is attractive, whatever their age, compared to someone with flabby arms or thighs. And with regular exercise and a healthy balanced diet, you'll look radiant and bursting with vitality. So don't risk squandering all your spare cash on going out clubbing and buying new clothes; prioritise what you spend on your health and fitness.

2

What's your drinking rate? Your liver can process one unit of alcohol an hour. Stick to that and fill up with water for the rest of the time. You'll find you feel more in control, you may never have a hangover again and you'll have more energy the next day.

3

On a piece of paper write the following: eat no more than 6 g of salt a day; eat 5 or more portions of fruit and vegetables a day; be active for at least 30 minutes at least 5 days a week; drink no more than safe recommended amounts of alcohol; achieve my ideal weight. Tick each one that you are already achieving. Next, choose one that you're not doing but you aim to tick off next. That's all you have to do.

4

Getting to the gym can be made into part of your workout routine if you treat it as a warm-up. If you drive to the gym, then park further away and walk the last five minutes. If you take a bus or tube, then get off at the stop before. If you walk briskly and change fast, then your pulse and body temperature should still be above normal and you should be more ready for action.

5

Get a good breakfast in! A recent study revealed that people who didn't eat breakfast were more likely to be overweight and less intelligent. So, if you didn't have a good reason before, you have now. A good breakfast will sustain you through to lunch, but remember that sugary cereals will pick you up and then drop you like a stone.

6

Be more active around the house. If you're downstairs use the toilet upstairs, and vice versa. Move up the stairs briskly. Get up to answer the phone and walk around while talking. Open the door yourself rather than buzzing the person in through the entry phone. You'll be surprised how easy it is to do these simple but effective activities.

7

Combining exercising and socialising will make the time you spend getting and staying fit more fun, then you'll be likely to stick with it. What about a regular bike ride with the family? Or link up with a few other cyclists and take it in turns to plan routes for the gang. Take up a regular salsa class or join in a weekly aerobics session; make new friends there, or take your friends along. If you're on a business trip, arrange a round of golf – that'll help with the networking and might clinch a deal, as well as doing you good.

8

Eat more slowly. It takes 20 minutes for 'I'm full' signals to reach the brain. Work with your body by giving it the time it needs to respond.

9

'The lift' is a Pilates exercise you can do at your office chair or on the bus. The aim is to work on zipping up from the bottom of the pelvis towards your ribs. While sitting upright, imagine that there is a lift on your pelvic floor. As you breathe out try to take that lift 'up' to the next floor – you should feel your pelvic muscles go taut. As you take the 'lift' further up the floors from 'first' to 'second', you should feel your lower abdominals tighten.

10

Keep a great variety of foods in the fridge for making packed lunches. Taking your lunch to work with you will help to reduce temptation – no chips or burgers for you from the canteen, or fattening sandwiches. Instead, perhaps, healthy strips of lean ham, or pieces of tuna with a salad or crispbread, all accompanied by fruit, yoghurt, a light cheese spread and bread sticks…

11

Here's a simple way of checking your fitness level. Find your resting heart rate by taking your pulse in the morning before you get up. Press your fingers (not your thumb) on the main artery in the side of your neck, just below the jawbone. Using a watch with a second hand or a stopwatch, count the number of heartbeats in six seconds. Multiply this by ten to get your resting heart rate. Now, step up and down on a step or low bench, alternately leading legs for three minutes. Rest for thirty seconds then take your pulse for six seconds and multiply the result by ten. This is your recovery heart rate.

The nearer it is to your resting heart rate, the fitter you are. If it takes more than ten minutes to return to your normal rate, your fitness level needs attention.

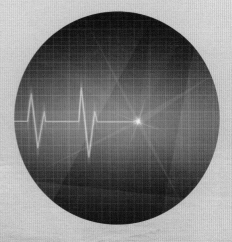

12

What's the simplest way to add more healthy years to your life? Drink more water. Drink more than five glasses a day and you'll halve your risk of certain cancers. But according to one recent survey, most of us drink fewer than four glasses of water every day. Why not buy a filter jug that fits in the fridge? Then you'll have cool, clean tasting water 'on tap'. Aim for two litres (around ten glasses) a day.

13

List all the positive habits that you'd like to incorporate into your life, then add in just one new habit a week. Start with an easy one first, such as getting up 10 minutes earlier each day. Then the following week add another, like 10 minutes of stretching. Tick off each habit as you incorporate it into your schedule and once you've done four, give yourself a small reward like a trip somewhere nice. The following month add another four new habits, and so on.

14

Dancing is both a great way to burn off those calories and a great de-stressor, so get out there and strut your stuff. Added bonuses are meeting people and forgetting about any worries for an entire evening!

15

Why not opt for a Mediterranean diet? That'll have olive oil, grains and cereals, pasta, fruits, vegetables and legumes, limited amounts of eggs and dairy products, some fish and poultry, and even some wine in moderation. A diet like this is high in retinoids, folic acid and fibre, which helps prevent heart disease. An added bonus for your health is that having a high level of folic acid in your diet also protects you against colon cancer and dementia!

16

Try conjuring up an image of yourself as you'd like to be in a year's time. Someone who enjoys exercising three times a week, cooks imaginative, healthy dishes and has a fulfilling social life? Someone who's 12 kg lighter, who's given up smoking and who sticks to 14 units (or 21 if you're a man) of alcohol a week? Write down weekly steps that will get you to your goal. This week, it could be buying a new recipe book and learning to cook with pulses. Next week, it could be joining a local running group.

17

Make your swimming stroke more efficient by taking up a new sport – stroke golf. Swim a length and count the number of strokes it takes you to complete it. Now try to swim the length using fewer strokes. See how far you can bring down your score by concentrating on getting the most progress out of the smallest number of strokes.

18

Try to eat at least five portions of fruit and vegetables daily. And the more colours the better – try red peppers, yellow peppers, green peppers, red cabbage, sweet potatoes, etc. This way you can get plenty of antioxidants.

19

Exercise your ankle and shins anytime and anywhere. Kick your shoes off and slowly write the entire alphabet, letter by letter, with your toes on the floor. Drawing every letter will have you bending your foot pretty much every which way. Of course if you happen to be an Arabic or Mandarin writer, then you're going to end up with shins like Stallone's biceps. When you've finished don't forget to repeat the sequence with the other foot. As well as exercising your shin muscles, playing footsie is a great little stress buster and highly recommended if you're stuck behind a desk.

20

Find a friend who also needs or wants to get fit. Decide together what exercise you'd both like to do. Each time you do it you award yourself a point. The one who scores the least at the end of the week pays for an evening out – a meal, a movie or the beer tab. This isn't a particularly serious challenge, but it's fun and is motivating. It's up to you what level of challenge you set and what your reward is.

21

Don't forget to chew! Unchewed food is hard to digest and its micronutrients pass through our systems. The less you chew your superfoods, the less their micronutrients are absorbed. Aim to chew each mouthful fifteen times before swallowing.

22

Try water running. If you can get a moment when the pool isn't packed, try walking or running up and down the lanes of the pool to get a feel for the resistance. If you can 'run' in water up to your thighs, then so much the better – try to concentrate on lifting your knees high with every step. You'll use around double the calories to run or walk for the same time you would on dry land.

23

If you're really determined to lose weight, why not really focus on it for a week? Start as you mean to go on and bin unhealthy packages lurking in your cupboards and fridge. Then get hold of the right ingredients: fresh foods and basic dry ingredients like lentils, chickpeas and brown rice. Have a breakfast of porridge with fresh fruit and yoghurt, or eggs on rye toast. For lunch try a great big salad with all the trimmings, but go easy on the dressing – just a little olive oil and lemon juice. End your day with something like grilled fish and broccoli. If you get hungry, a small protein snack will help – nuts and seeds are useful.

24

Not sure if you're exceeding the recommended weekly alcohol limits of 14 units for women and 21 for men? Then try keeping a drink diary for a week. You may be surprised at how quickly your units add up.

25

Eat two bananas a day. Have one for breakfast and one as a mid-afternoon snack. This way if you are someone who doesn't usually have breakfast you'll find how easy it is to do so. The mid-afternoon snack banana will help you overcome that end-of-the-day sluggish feeling. And you'll be helping to keep your blood pressure healthy, without any effort.

26

If you don't know what your cholesterol level is, make an appointment with your doctor to get tested this week. Alternatively buy a cholesterol self-test from pharmacies which involves taking a small sample of blood from your finger tip and placing it on a test strip. Results are then compared to a colour chart in three minutes.

27

A lot of salsa clubs offer a deal combining a lesson and a night on the tiles. You show up for an hour or so before the club opens and have a refresher lesson in form or perhaps a new move or two. Because it's still early you then get to practice while the club is fairly empty, and most of the other people there will be the same dancers you met in the hour-long class. Not only have you already met but you are all there to learn so it makes finding partners much easier. By the time the club fills up you should be much less self-conscious and ready to show them what you're made of.

28

How can you get five fruit and vegetables into your daily diet? Try having one piece of fruit at breakfast, plus a piece of fruit after lunch or as an afternoon snack; have a salad with lunch or dinner and two vegetables (not potatoes) with your other meal.

29

Not sure exactly how much sleep you need? Here's an easy way to find out. Set your alarm for when you need to get up, then count back six to eight hours, depending on how much sleep you feel you need. Try to go to bed at this time every night, and get up at the same time – even at weekends. If you still feel tired during the day, push your bedtime back by fifteen minutes a week until you wake up feeling refreshed.

31

Try a boxer's workout. Skip for three minutes (the time of a round) then perform as many crunches as you can for a minute. Now skip for three minutes again, then perform as many press-ups as you can in a minute. Skip again for three minutes, then a minute of crunches. Repeat until you've worked out for half an hour. That should have worked out your speed, endurance, upper and lower body strength. The skipping means that your heartrate should remain significantly higher than usual even during the one-minute press up/crunch 'breaks' so it's a full half hour of cardio exercise.

30

To lose weight try reducing your meal portion size. If you are cooking for yourself, cut your servings by around 25%. If eating out, try the children's meal, or if you're with a friend, then share a meal. This will reduce your calorie intake and you will feel satisfied rather than uncomfortable.

32

Do just one thing today to improve your health. Add a piece of fruit to your diet, go for a walk or get to a yoga class. Keep up that change for one month, which should be enough to make it a permanent habit.

33

Having a running partner can make all the difference. It can make time fly as you chat, turn a fitness effort into 'quality time' with friends or family and it can help motivate you to show up in the first place. Look online and in local papers for running clubs. Many gyms also have groups of runners and they'll often be happy for newcomers to join regardless of whether or not you're a member.

34

Regular massage not only reduces stress and anxiety, it can also boost the immune system by increasing levels of infection-fighting cells. Can't coerce someone into doing it? Don't have the time or spare cash to see a professional? No problem – simply get a tennis ball, lean against a wall and roll the ball around between your back and shoulders and the wall. Try it – you'll be hooked.

35

You can eat your fluids, too. Fruit and vegetables are largely water – apricots, grapes, melons, peaches, strawberries, cucumbers, mangoes, oranges and peppers all comprise over 75% water. Fish such as sardines, mackerel, salmon and tuna are also 50% water.

36

When it comes to abs what most of us want is tone rather than size or strength and a lot of that comes not from how developed the muscle is, but how taut it is. The key to tautness is keeping those abs contracted throughout exercises, and indeed throughout the day. One approach is to tie a piece of string around your waist (under your clothes of course) so that if you let your belly out it will touch the string. The idea is that it becomes a subconscious reminder and whenever your tum touches the string it makes you pull it in, effectively exercising your abs all day long.

37

You'll sleep better with exercise. Being tired might seem essential to promoting good sleep, but it doesn't necessarily work like that; you can lie staring at the ceiling for ages. It's got to be the right sort of tired, exhaustion from physical rather than mental exercise. So get at least four to six hours of moderate exercise a week and your sleep should improve. That's only a matter of a fifteen-minute walk a day in the morning and again in the evening with a few more trips up and down the stairs.

38

Experts now recommend that people eat at least two portions of fish a week, one of which should be oily. During the next week have one portion of oily fish. The following week have two portions of fish, one oily and one white fish such as cod, haddock or plaice.

39

Try these easy press ups. Stand facing a wall with your arms shoulder-width apart. With hands on the wall slowly fall towards it and then push yourself back with your arms. Repeat this 35 times: it's a great way to keep the upper body trim without falling flat on your face whilst trying to do a press-up.

40

Put the remote out of reach. Somewhere where it's quicker for you to get up and manually change channels. Soon doing this will become a habit, you'll be changing channels like in the old days, and helping your blood pressure into the bargain.

41

Write down how many steps you think you take during each day of the week. Then get a pedometer and see how close you were with your estimate and how close you are to the 10,000 steps a day target. If you're already there, congratulations! Now try increasing the target by 500 steps each week. If you're not quite there yet, keep on trying.

42

Calculate your body mass index. Weigh yourself in kilograms (W). Measure your height in metres (H). Divide your weight in kilograms (W) by your height in metres (H), and divide this by your height in metres (H) again. And voilà, the result is your BMI. You can do this in your head or use a calculator.

43

If cycling gets your wheels turning consider combining it with a holiday. Find a company that'll give you an itinerary suited to your energy level plus accompanying cars to drop off your baggage at the next hotel on the route, then all you'll have to do is pedal and enjoy the view.

2

be arsed...
to supercharge your career
(you have to work at it)

44

Think about what you find most rewarding at work. One of the enormous but unspoken realities of life is that most people are basically bored by their jobs. What you value most will probably be to do with your achievements, others recognising your good work, feeling a sense of responsibility or ownership for your work, seeing your career advance and realising that you're growing as a person. Once you know what motivates you, check the extent to which these things are part of your current job. If there's little match, start scanning those job ads now.

45

By using recruitment agencies, the internet and the HR department you should be able to work out the top and bottom ends of the sort of salary someone in your position gets. Now work out why you deserve to be in the top 25% of the band. When you have a good case, take it to your boss. If you are already in the top quartile, look for a promotion.

46

When applying for a job, try this test on the first draft of your CV. Highlight in green the lines you think positively sell you against the specific vacancy you're applying for. Use yellow to highlight any 'neutral' information that neither sells nor harms you. And then red for anything that the recruiter might consider negative or problematic. What does the balance of shadings tell you?

47

Have a look at your last appraisal. Is there anything there you can use as proof that someone else has noted your natural abilities in the leadership area? It's always more powerful to quote someone else than point out, modestly of course, how brilliant you think you are.

48

Thinking of a career change?
Phone a friend – or three. You
almost certainly know people
who have transferred skills and
started working in another career.
Pick their brains on how they
financed it, got their family on
side, garnered the qualifications,
coped with problems. Those who
have pursued their happiness are
going to have more practical
advice, on coping with the
good and bad, as well as
more enthusiasm than
those who haven't taken
a similar leap.

49

Make a regular plan for staying in
contact with a wide range of people
in your address book. Not a circular
letter at Christmas; just a personal
note asking how they are doing.
This keeps your name alive, triggers
thoughts and will give rise to all
sorts of opportunities.

50

Before a job interview, go over your CV with a fine toothcomb. Challenge yourself to substantiate every claim you've made. If you feel that funnel questioning will catch you out, change the wording. You won't necessarily weaken your case and you remove the risk of looking as though you were trying to pull the wool over their eyes.

51

Most people wait to have their authority increased before they take on new responsibilities. This is slow-lane career thinking. Find something in your organisation that needs fixing and just do it. If you don't have the authority and your action plainly has a good result then you have probably expanded your responsibilities. (You may have to smooth a few ruffled feathers, but so what?)

52

Make a list of your career priorities for the next six months. Then put an entry in your diary for six months from today, marking it something like 'Personal Review', and on that date allow yourself at least a couple of hours to take stock of how you got on. Make this an ongoing process.

53

Looking to get on the first rung of the career ladder? A run-of-the-mill job can look good on your CV. You can learn a lot from that part-time job in retail or behind a bar. Okay, it's not as glamorous as an internship with a leading computer firm, but you can spell out how it gave you early responsibility. Did it help hone your customer service skills? Did you deal with return of goods when the manager was off sick? Did you organise and promote musical events at the pub where you worked? It's how you make what you do count that interests graduate recruiters.

55

Pick your time to call. Did you know you have a much better chance of getting hold of a contact between 8.30 and 10.00 in the morning or after 4.30 in the afternoon? At these times people are less likely to be busy with routine tasks or away from their desks at meetings. As a result they are more likely to pick up the phone because it's more convenient for them to talk.

54

Look closely at what your customer is trying to achieve. Look at what their competitors are doing. Study their trade press. Talk to other people in your organisation who provide similar products and services to their customers. Use the internet. From that research, come up with an innovative idea to take to the customer.

56

If a goal appears to be too big and intimidating to tackle, resist the temptation to run away and hide and instead try to break it into bite-sized chunks. First look at the whole huge scary dream and do a five-year vision, based on where you dream of being. Do you see yourself in that corner office on Wall Street or relaxing on the beach with your two kids? If you fancy the latter, you'd better get yourself into gear and start earning more money. Ask yourself what you need to do to achieve that. Can you earn more in your present job? Do you need to change jobs? Should you start your own company? Once you've figured out what you need to do to achieve your big goal, list just one thing you could do today to get there, however small.

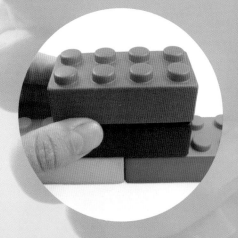

57

Be proactive with the job you want; don't wait for the job advertisement which is looking for you. Try and create the role of your dreams where you are, or contact organisations who have such a role. Write, ring and propose. If you are truly passionate about that role it will come across and the role will be yours. Don't expect instant success; keep trying and be willing to take intermediate positions to help you build experience.

58

For speculative job applications, always find a named person to write to. Anything addressed to 'The Personnel Manager' or opening with 'Dear Sir/Madam' is liable to end up on the desk of an admin underling. If, on the other hand, you write to an individual personally, you'll turn the epistolary equivalent of a cold call into a much warmer approach.

59

Become the company scout. Sniffing out the competition is a great way to keep your eye on new opportunities. You may raise eyebrows within your own company but it's actually useful for them to know what their rivals are doing. Position yourself to take part in industry events like conferences and seminars where you'll meet your opposite numbers from companies in your sector.

60

Take your business. Take a couple of your competitors. Finally take a few companies who have some similarities, maybe size or geography or business model. Be absolutely ruthless. What are they doing that you believe makes them successful and that you are not doing, what ways of working could you learn from them? Whether it's a coffee shop being open at 6.30 a.m. instead of 8.00 a.m., a publisher running a blog giving free chapter samples or a dentist offering the first inspection free – it's worth trying. Identify five immediate 'modelling excellence' actions that you can take.

61

Start as you mean to go on. Before you enter the premises on your first day of a new job, take a moment to compose yourself. Stretch your spine, drop your shoulders and relax your facial muscles to relieve tension. Now stride in as confidently as you can. Greet everyone with a warm, friendly smile and a firm handshake. You may still feel incredibly nervous but you're off to a great start.

62

Boost work morale in a stressful workplace by starting group traditions beyond getting drunk on Friday night and moaning. Go out for a Chinese on pay day or book an awayday at a spa or have a whip-round every birthday and celebrate with champagne and cake.

63

Find something difficult that needs to be done, some major change that the organisation needs to make. Perhaps your boss hasn't thought of it or has thought it too tough, but he or she would be happy to take the credit for it. Offer to manage it, and deliver.

64

Think about times in your career when you've been very successful and enjoyed the job at the same time. Now think about the culture you were working in. What was it about the culture that contributed to those good feelings? Now try the opposite – when you were miserable. Comparing the two should help to uncover the environment in which you really like working.

65

Get a copy of your annual report and the annual report of your main competitor. Do some financial analysis of the two companies and see who is in the better state and why. If you cannot do this, go and see a friendly financial controller and ask them to help you, and give you some advice about how to improve your financial awareness.

66

Write down the half-a-dozen or so networks of which you are already a member – use a separate sheet of paper for each one. Then list individuals in each network and how that contact might be able to help you (e.g. with information or an introduction that could take you nearer your next career goal). These are the people you need to get in touch with – the more of them you talk to, the more likely you are to make progress.

67

You need an A4 piece of paper. Rule a line down the middle vertically. Head the left-hand column with SAME and the right with DIFFERENT. Now write about yourself, assigning your assets to one of the columns. So in SAME you might put 'same degree and vocational qualifications as rest of team'; in DIFFERENT you might have 'highly engaging presenter; unusual ability to understand a profit and loss account at speed'. You'll guess the purpose of this, I'm sure: you need plenty of things in the DIFFERENT column. Discover them or create them: your choice!

68

If you want to arrive late to and/or leave early from a meeting, keep one of those small suitcases with wheels on it and bring it to the meeting. Quietly park it in plain view. A late arrival means you just got off a plane or train. An early departure means that you really have to get to the airport or station right away. Your very presence will seem like you're doing everyone a favour.

69

If you have a boss who takes credit for your ideas, get your retaliation in first. Let others know about your bright ideas, especially senior management. Put your name on the cover of your proposals to make sure your prior claim is documented. Then, if your idea turns out to be a winner, tell your boss's boss how grateful you were for your boss's encouragement – even if they haven't helped at all. This avoids annoying your boss and makes you look like a star team player.

70

Develop a 'personal recovery plan' to enable you to cope more effectively in the event of your job/primary source of income disappearing tomorrow. What would you do? How would you pay the rent/mortgage? Is this an opportunity for a career change?

71

When did you last meet the most senior person in your building? If you are not based at the company's headquarters the answer to that question has to be at least in the last month. Take responsibility for this – do you know when you will next have an opportunity to meet senior people?

72

Think about what you can delegate. We're not just talking about giving some more of your paperwork to an assistant – they are probably overworked, too. Can your mother collect the kids from school now and again? Can you order your groceries online instead of visiting the shops? How about outsourcing some of the household chores, like ironing, to a friend, student or neighbour? These services will cost you something but is doing these petty chores more important than fulfilling your ambitions?

73

When applying for a job, be explicit about how you meet the specification in your covering letter. If the advertisement asks for somebody who can do A, B and C, then your covering letter should detail how A, B and C are the very things you do best.

74

At your boss's next team meeting don't leap in with your views. Listen until everyone has spoken, assimilate what has been said and eventually summarise the substance. By that time you will know where your interests lie and be able to steer the meeting towards them.

75

Your seniors will pay more attention to a customer who praises you than to anyone else. So make it happen. When something has gone well, and assuming you have a close relationship with your customer, get them to write a thank-you note to you, copied to the most senior person they know in your organisation, preferably at least your boss's boss. Time this to coincide with another key event, your appraisal maybe, or your big request for more resources. But don't overdo it or your boss will know that it is you setting it up.

76

Instead of sending an email, say it in person. It's easy to confuse efficiency with effectiveness: just because you have sent an email doesn't mean you have dealt with something. Talking face-to-face helps move things along faster, especially if you have something tricky to discuss. Before you fire off your next reply, think whether it might be quicker in the long run to say it in person.

77

Conduct your next meeting standing up. Studies show that conversations between people who are standing are significantly shorter than those between people who are sitting down. People perceive a person standing up at a meeting to have higher status than those who sit. Decisions tend to be quicker and meeting times shorter, a huge cost saving in terms of people's time, especially if expensive lawyers and bankers are charging by the hour.

78

Make it clear to colleagues past and present that you're very happy to provide a reference for them. This will both earn you their gratitude and help you to keep tabs on who is moving where. In so doing you'll provide yourself with a range of networking contacts in different organisations.

79

It's absolutely true that if you look for unlikely opportunities in your working life they are likely to happen. Whenever you are talking to or listening to senior people try to find an angle where you can help. Listen for a statement like, 'we need to look into this' or words to that effect. Do a bit of research on the topic in question and send it to them with an offer to find out more.

80

Be public spirited. Doing something on top of your work or home life can help you stand out from the competition. Join a public body or become a school governor. The bonus is that public bodies have to be accountable – they have to publish information about their activities and membership. This means that someone doing an online search for background information on you will come across your name in relation to your public duties, which could give you an edge in career situations.

81

If you're leaving, make life as easy as possible for whoever takes over your responsibilities. It will enhance your professional reputation. So, finish off as much of your current workload as possible. What you can't finish, you must hand over professionally. Prepare a handover document, which will bring your successor instantly up to speed. It should include a status report on unfinished business, contact information and any useful tips that will help, such as the next steps on a project.

82

Look around at how you and your colleagues work. Now ask yourself this question: 'If I owned this business, what changes would I make to my part of the organisation to make a big improvement?' This should give you loads of ammunition to suggest the changes which sensibly should be made. Now you're off and running towards inventing and then taking the new job that you really want.

83

Make sure you're applying for the right jobs. If the same lack of knowledge or experience keeps stopping you getting jobs, you'll have to do something radical about it or work out an alternative route to getting where you want to be. It's never a good idea to keep banging your head against a brick wall. The best people to help you understand the real problem are those who've interviewed you and not selected you. Ask all of them for feedback in the specific area where they felt your knowledge and experience let you down. Talk to them about whether and how you could put it right.

3

be arsed...
to look your best
(and turn some heads)

84

Get a fake tan. It can make you look slimmer and leaner by sculpting, shadowing and highlighting muscles and curves. For the best results, have it applied in a salon. It will usually last for about five days.

85

Try an instant image change with a haircut. Layers can make your face look slimmer as can highlights. For men, a short, sharp haircut can make you look more George Clooney than Billy Bunter. Great hair works wonders.

86

To curb your appetite, chew sugar-free gum or clean your teeth after a meal or a snack. As well as cleaning your teeth and giving you sweet breath, it sends you a psychological message that you have finished eating and that it is time to do something else. Make a clean break when your meal ends so that you really know that it is over.

87

Ladies, try brushing shimmery bronzer on the backs of legs or thighs or smother thighs with a light-reflecting cream or lotion. They catch the light, making legs look smoother and draw attention away from the cellulitey bits.

88

Go through your wardrobe and throw away anything that is baggy and shapeless or too tight. Try on doubtful items and take a long hard look at yourself in the mirror. Does it flatter you? Any doubts, chuck it out.

89

Improving your posture can make you look slimmer instantly. Relax your shoulders and draw them down and slightly back. Your chest should then naturally lift. Investigate Pilates or Alexander technique classes for more posture skills.

90

Green tea can raise the metabolic rate. If you drink four or five cups a day, you could burn up around 70 calories – for doing very little! Drinking green tea could lose you nearly half a stone over a year. Put the kettle on!

91

If you're going out to a club, you don't have to dress up elaborately in uncomfortable clothes. You're going out to enjoy yourself. Dress casual, be yourself, wear clothes that don't involve sucking in your belly and which you can work up a sweat in. If other people want to dress like corseted peacocks, let them.

92

Write down the five things that most attract you to someone. And then work out how you can adapt them to work for you. For example, someone might have a very sexy tone of voice that you could imitate or maybe a way of sitting that is attractive. Practise small things like this and you'll already feel sexier and more confident.

93

Sort your clothes in your wardrobe properly – separate the winter clothes from the summer clothes, solids from patterns, neutrals from bright colours. It makes assembling an outfit quicker, and shows up where you're missing an essential item. Most important of all, a good wardrobe keeps your clothes clean and crease-free. If you don't have a wardrobe that's big enough for this task, buy one before you buy anything else.

94

If you are toned you will never look out of shape, no matter how voluptuous you are. You should do sit-ups, press-ups and bottom clenches every day. Hone those beautiful curves until they are irresistibly perfect.

95

Maximise your lips. To pout beautifully, turn to the camera and say 'Wogan'. Bizarre, maybe, but glamour models swear by it.

96

Couch potatoes can turn an evening vegging in front of the TV into a workout by fidgeting more, which can apparently burn up to 800 calories a day. So make a point of shifting around every fifteen minutes – adjust your posture, roll your shoulders or change the way you cross your legs. The same goes for sitting at your desk or driving.

97

Try to have one or two days a week when you eat only raw foods to spring clean your system and help the detoxification process. It's easier and tastier than it sounds - think enormous platefuls of all your favourite salad ingredients, including avocado, sprinkled with fresh aromatic herbs; loads of fruit; snacks of nuts and freshly squeezed juices. By definition eating raw foods makes it impossible to consume any processed, fatty or sugary foods, helps you to lose weight and fills you up with first-class nutrients - raw fruit and vegetables retain more vitamins than those that have been cooked.

98

Give yourself a facial workout to help tone your facial muscles and delay the ageing process. Stand in front of the mirror daily and raise your eyebrows as high as possible and simultaneously open your eyes as wide as you can. Slowly lower your eyebrows and relax. Repeat this five times.

99

A good exfoliation of the cellulite-prone areas of your bottom, thighs or upper arms will make the skin look a whole lot better. Give your skin a healthy, rosy glow by using an exfoliator at least twice a week when you're in the shower. Whether you choose one from the luxury body care ranges or a budget buy, you'll notice the difference immediately.

100

When you smile try to project the feeling of 'I'm so happy to be here talking to you' in a totally natural way, of course. Someone who seems to take genuine delight in your presence is almost impossible to resist.

101

To look your best when walking, check your posture. Aim to keep your shoulders back and your ribcage lifted. Pull your abdominal muscles in and think tall. Look forward not down. Strike forward with your heel and push off with your back foot. You can gradually increase the length of your stride but don't overstretch.

102

To be as stylish as a Parisienne, the devil is in the detail so you must not skimp on accessories. Always buy the most expensive handbag and shoes you can. A scarf of course is de rigeur, as is the little black dress. Try to make sure you have the basics in your wardrobe and that they are good quality; the rest will follow and you will look chic and sexy effortlessly.

103

Start wearing sunscreen on your face every day. Most (80%) of the lines and wrinkles you see in the mirror are caused by the sun but it's never too late to prevent more damage. We now know it's the sun's UVA, or non-burning, rays that age the skin, which means you're affected even in winter. Many daily moisturisers now include sun protective ingredients – just make sure you opt for one that's 'broad spectrum', to block out both UVA and UVB rays. In summer months, wear a sunscreen specially formulated for the face instead.

104

To lose weight, play with plate size. If you eat from an enormous plate, chances are you'll fill it with an enormous portion or feel short-changed because there doesn't appear to be much on it! Choosing a smaller plate and piling it up is a sneaky way to trick yourself that you're having a big meal.

105

If your hair's looking dull, take a close look at your diet. Be sure to eat plenty of protein-rich foods, such as lean meat, fish, tofu and dairy products, to encourage healthy hair growth. Also eat plenty of red meat, green leafy vegetables, eggs and fortified breakfast cereals, as hair loss is linked to a deficiency in iron.

106

Drinking two litres of still water a day can help your body burn off an extra 150 calories according to one study. It's thought to stimulate the sympathetic nervous system and increase the metabolic rate.

107

Get some perspective and start looking up rather than down! Stop spending so much of your time thinking about the past and future and looking down at your boots. Spend a day looking up instead and see how much more positive you feel about life. Look at your body and how you're holding yourself. Stop slouching otherwise you'll feel like a slouch. Stand up tall, put your shoulders back and smile. Acting as if you were confident will work quickly and effectively to elevate your self-esteem.

108

Eyedrops that get rid of blood shot eyes are your quickest route to a re-energised look. For ladies, navy eyeliner is the second quickest. It neutralizes 'red eye syndrome' better than black or brown and makes the whites of the eyes zing. On the whole keep make-up to the upper lids and lashes. The eyes of people looking at you will be dragged upwards, away from sagging.

109

If you want to look your best while posing for holiday snaps, hold yourself in a way that disguises excess curves; stand up and pivot slightly on your feet so your body including your shoulders is at a slight angle. Put your hands on your hips to make your waist look smaller. Overall it'll take inches off your body.

110

Get some glamorous photos taken of you (if necessary by a professional) and keep a few of them framed, in your bedroom. This is to remind you that you are sexy, and the better the photo the more confidence you'll feel. After all, glam shots in magazines are hardly simple snapshots!

be arsed...
to do something with your free time
(step 1: switch off the tv)

4

111

Keep a log of your TV viewing time over a week. If you watch TV for more than four hours a day, you'll eat more calories than you need to because you'll have more opportunity to snack and you'll burn fewer calories while you are still.

112

Don't hesitate! Start learning a new craft today. Whether you learn from a fellow practitioner one-to-one, enrol in a night class or buy a compendium book of crafts, pay your imagination the compliment of a complementary discipline through which to express itself.

113

Make a wish list that includes all the things you enjoy. You know – the things you say "I never have time for… these days". There's a good chance that many of them will only take you half an hour, so find a way to allow yourself that extra time. Make an appointment with yourself – write it in your diary – and go for a long walk, meditate, have an aromatherapy bath or a quick facial or a manicure. You could even find time to write a chapter of that novel you've always intended to produce.

114

Discover your roots. Local record offices can cover the whole spectrum of family and local history, and experienced staff are available to help you and make your search a success. If your family came from the area in which you now live, or you have a particular family or place (pub, park, school) that interests you, then make a visit to your local record office (check the opening times before you go). There the staff will guide you to deeds, maps, photographs, possibly copies of the Victorian census returns and much else. You will be amazed what you can discover.

115

Printing with potatoes is a quick, simple way of exploring the recurring elements of pattern – it really is wasted on young children! Cut a raw potato in half and carve your design out of the exposed face. Apply poster paint to your motif with a brush, and press it gently onto a sheet of paper. Now, can you make a complementary pattern from the other half of the potato? Try making a border frieze for a poster, or an image for next year's Christmas cards.

116

Have a good de-cluttering session. Take some photographs before and after you begin the process to demonstrate the amazing impact that the exercise can have on a room.

117

Be inspired to write a story. Open your eyes and look around you. There is material everywhere. Read old diaries, newspapers and magazines for fascinating stories. Sit in a café and gaze out of the window. Listen to conversations, invent stories for the people who walk past and write them down. It may take a while, but if you pay attention to the world around you, then inspiration will come. The trick is not to go looking for the idea of a lifetime. Sit back, relax, soak up your surroundings, listen to the scraps of thought that flutter through your brain and before you know it you'll be running round the block screaming 'Eureka!'.

118

Grow your own sweet chestnuts. Collect plump, ripe healthy-looking nuts in autumn. Remove the spiky casings and then float them in water. Only the nuts that sink are viable, so pot them up immediately but don't forget to give them some protection from both frost and the squirrels.

119

Pick a wall or a shelf in your home to be a gallery space for your own creations. Change the exhibition regularly, say every month. If you share the place with anyone, take it in turns with them to select the next month's display – that way, every other month you will have the extra pleasure of surprise, and it is bound to trigger some interesting discussions about sources of inspiration as well as techniques to try.

121

Make a mask! On a balloon larger than your own head, tape a nose shape (e.g. an equilateral triangle folded in half) in roughly the right place, to protect a space for your nose in the finished mask. Tape the balloon down, nose uppermost, to stop it rolling away. Now layer papier maché strips to a depth of 2-3mm (in) over the whole area of the face and beyond. Let it dry hard, then remove the balloon (go on, burst it!) and trim the mask to shape with scissors. Cut out eye holes now too, using the nose cavity to decide position. Now build up facial features, decorate, and prepare to be transformed.

120

Decorate your garden with outdoor fairy lights. They look great wrapped round the trunk of a tree or draped over a trellis, especially during the festive season. Ropes of lights are also effective, just twisting through your borders or lighting up the outline of a garden structure.

Get some gardening inspiration from other gardens, whether big or small. Many villages organise garden strolls – not to mention the National Garden Scheme, which lists gardens open for charity in its infamous Yellow Book.

If you can't find the thing that sparks your imagination and promises to cater for your interest locally, sound out your friends, family and neighbours. If enough of them are keen on your bright idea you can start with a small meeting at home for no cost at all. If it's a success you can organise the next meeting in the community centre and charge everyone a small fee to cover the cost.

124

If you want a cheap-and-cheerful version of horseracing, go to the dogs. Many of our greyhound stadia are under threat which is sad because they can be excellent atmospheric places. Most have little restaurants with a view of the finish line where you can get a meal and a drink, and people come to your table to take your bets. Entry prices are cheap and anyone can understand what's going on - so they're good for the kids too.

125

Try out some different wines. Good sources of unusual wines are restaurants that specialise in offbeat cuisine such as German, Lebanese or Swiss. Good Greek, Cypriot and Turkish restaurants also tend to have a good selection of wines from the Mediterranean. Most of these specialist restaurants are likely to have wines that it would be almost impossible to buy anywhere else. These restaurants will also give you the opportunity to taste the wines in a gastronomic context where they might not taste quite so weird.

126

Turn household objects into art. Take glass flower arranging beads for example. Fill two or three plain, straight-sided vases with a variety of different coloured beads and group them together along a window sill – when the light catches them they look amazing.

127

Take up creative writing. For academic courses, visit the websites of colleges and universities. Adult education colleges also often offer workshops. Contact your regional arts association for a list of writers' groups in your area open to newcomers or ask local people if they know of any good groups. If all of the above fails, start your own group with any writers you know.

Take your camera to a place where people or animals move – for example a public park, a bird table or a sports ground. Spend an hour or two capturing movement in as many photographs as you can. Don't think – just snap! When you have downloaded the results to your computer, see how they capture not just the physical process of movement but also the aesthetic sense of it: the blur of a wing, the odd angle of a foot as it steps off. Next day, return to the same place with a sketchbook and pencil and use your new camera-assisted insight to draw the same movements.

Today, and every day from now one, set aside a small period of time – anything from ten minutes to an hour – and do something you enjoy. It could be serious fun (roller-blading down the High Street?) or it could be something really small. It doesn't matter what it is – go window shopping; cuddle the cat; kick leaves – just try for something different every day and, when you do it, do it one hundred percent. Concentrate entirely on your chosen activity, and for a few minutes' play you'll get a day's worth of that heady feeling that tells you life's worth living.

130

Don't get bogged down by some outdated, teacher-engendered view of yourself as 'not artistic'. Allow yourself to explore a variety of different types of creative activity. Book yourself on some taster courses at the local college or community centre, or look at books in the library to find something that inspires you. Remember, it doesn't have to be traditional art: it could be weaving, cooking, web design, graphics, garden design – whatever takes your fancy. Don't forget to look online for inspiration too.

131

Grow your own vegetables. Growing veg from seed is time consuming, so why not buy some young vegetable plants. Go for healthy, stocky plants but don't buy until the frosts have passed, unless you've a greenhouse to protect them.

132

Turn your next pub crawl into an heraldic adventure by only visiting those hostelries named after coats-of-arms or badges or other elements taken from the world of heraldry: The Kings Arms, The White Hart, The Bear and Ragged Staff, The Feathers, The Wheatsheaf – you will find your own. Then see if you can find out why the pub is called what it is. For example, the Bear and Ragged Staff represents the Earl of Warwick, and the Feathers the Black Prince. The Wheatsheaf stands for bakers and horseshoes for blacksmiths.

133

How about a bit of architectural lawn sculpture? By setting the mower blades at differing levels you can cut a low-level maze or pattern into your lawn. Hours of fun, effective to look at, and easy to do.

Invent a board game. No inspiration? Well, a London cabbie recently hit the jackpot with a game based on The Knowledge. What a great idea! Use your expertise to devise your own game. Once you've got your idea, don't waste it - think through how the game will work and then make a prototype. User-test it with a few friends.

To get some inspiration for your home decor, visit a few luxury hotels. You don't have to stay, just go for a drink or for tea. While you are there make sure you examine every last detail to give you ideas. Creating the look and feel of luxury isn't necessarily about throwing money around – more often than not it is the result of plenty of thought and planning. What's more you're bound to enjoy the investigative experience!

5

be arsed...
to help the environment

(is it really all that hard
to sort your rubbish?)

136

Find out about organic producers near you and if there are any brown box schemes where locally grown seasonal food can be delivered regularly to your door. Don't be afraid to shop around as some are more expensive than others and quality can vary.

137

Turn your home eco-friendly. If it seems a bit daunting, why not carry out a mini audit one room at a time? Start with the smallest room in the house – the toilet! Every detail counts: is the loo roll recycled paper, are the light bulbs energy savers, are the cleaning materials toxic, how much water is flushed, is the tap water overheated, and even is the loo seat made from forest friendly wood from a certified source. It all has an impact. And from there, you can progress to the rest of the house.

138

Walking is one environmentally friendly sport you could take up today. You don't need any special equipment apart from a good pair of shoes, or any preparation as you can go at your own pace. Walking is low impact in all senses: it uses minimal resources, doesn't cost a penny and is gentle enough to suit all abilities. It's good for your heart, lungs, muscles and bone growth, and your feeling of wellbeing. People who walk regularly have reduced mortality rates, and up to half the risk of cardiovascular disease. Walkers are less anxious, sleep well and have better body weight control. Experts recommend 30 minutes of brisk walking daily.

139

Think before you flush. Toilets use about 30 per cent of the total water used in a household, and the older your cistern the more water you waste, with the worst offenders flushing away a whopping 13 litres of water each time you pull the plug! (Modern dual-flush toilets use six litres for a full flush and four litres with a 'mini' flush.) If your loo is more than a few years old, install a cistern displacement device, which is basically an inflated plastic bag that sits inside the cistern and displaces about one litre of water every time you flush. It doesn't sound like much, but when you think that the average household flushes up to 5000 times per year, that's an awful lot of water!

140

If you've only got room for one crop this year, make it courgette. Well known for its prolific cropping, this sure-fire summer squash is a doddle to cultivate from either seed or plant, and can even be grown in a pot. Cooked as a vegetable (though technically a fruit), organically grown courgettes have a light, sweet, slightly nutty flavour. They are a good source of vitamins A and C, potassium, antioxidants and fibre. You can use the colourful flowers in a variety of recipes: stuffed, sautéed, baked and in soup. The tubular green courgette is the most familiar, but colours range from black through various shades of grey, green, yellow and even white, and some varieties are round or bottle-shaped.

141

Host an organic wine tasting – enjoy yourself and spread the organic message at the same time. Get in a range of six or so red and white wines and invite some friends round; you don't even have to tell them the wines are organic (you can remove the labels – keep a list and number the bottles instead – and spring that one on them once they've realised how good they are). You'll probably find the after-effects of this kind of evening much less painful, too.

142

Learn how to read labels. It sounds simple, but consumers have little to go on beyond warnings on labels. If it has a big cross or toxicity warning, don't use it. Don't be misled by vague words such as 'natural' or 'botanical' or pictures of plants on labels. Many such products haven't even seen a whiff of a plant-based ingredient. Even if they do have a few drops of essential oils they tend to contain chemical nasties unless they expressly state that they don't. Learn to look for buzz words such as: plant-based, no nitrates, no phosphates, no chlorine, no petroleum products and no solvents.

143

If you're new to companion planting, you can't get a better friend than nasturtiums. These sunny, golden-orange flowers – a favourite of the painter Monet – can reduce your need for insecticides. When grown with ornamentals and vegetables, nasturtium makes a good aphid control in the garden as they attract them away from other plants. The flowers also attract hoverflies that feed on aphids. These flexible friends have another use: they make a good crop in themselves as their flowers, leaves and pickled seeds can all be added into a mixed salad to give colour, flavour and texture.

144

Try this as an exercise: spend one week shopping only at your neighbourhood's shops and markets, and see how different it makes you feel. Instead of the rushed, anonymous experience of racing round the supermarket aisles with a trolley, enjoy the shopkeeper's personal attention, tried and trusted goods and pride in their stock. Ask to look, feel, taste and smell, too – and leave the car behind if you can or share with a friend. Supermarkets may be cheaper to shop at than local retailers as they can use their mighty buying power, but give the little guys a chance too!

145

Save cash and reduce your home's plastic pile-up by joining a toy library. The advantages are plentiful, and they are usually very affordable, too. Toy libraries provide good quality educational and play items for loan, mainly for pre-school children, and have a range of items covering all aspects of growth and development. You also have access to books, DVDs, CDs and even Playstation games. Libraries are a hub of activity, and you can meet other parents and carers, share information and join in activities. And the great thing is that once your child is fed up of a certain toy, back it goes for someone else to enjoy, freeing up space for the next big hit!

146

Befriend your local greengrocer. They discard sackfuls of perfect composting material everyday. If you're not already doing your ecologically friendly bit make a start here.

147

Make your own organic mouthwash. Stir into a cup of water: a quarter of a teaspoon of baking soda, a drop of organic peppermint oil and a drop of organic tea-tree oil. Pour this into a clean jar and shake to blend; use as required. The tea-tree oil acts as an antiseptic and helps to fight gum disease and the bacteria that cause bad breath and plaque. Another alternative is a rosemary mouthwash. Boil two cups of water, adding a sprig of fresh mint, a sprig of rosemary (best crushed) and a teaspoon of anise seeds. It smells delicious as it heats; when it is cool, strain and use as necessary.

148

Get an idea of how much electricity your electronics on standby use up, by switching off everything else except the stuff you leave on standby and watch your electricity meter spin round for an hour. Take a KW unit reading and cost it from your last bill, then multiply it by 24 to see how much your standby appliances use up over just one day. Scary stuff …

149

Surf the Internet to find suppliers of organic skincare ranges. Many suppliers offer sample sachets free of charge so you can try before you buy. Others offer free samples of a variety of products with a minimum purchase, and many offer small sample pots so you can try a product without splashing out on a full-size pot. Check out what's available, and ask if nothing is offered. Thy can only say no…

150

Help yourself to a restful night's sleep by using organic herbs. Valerian (Valeriana officinalis), passionflower (Passiflora incarnata) and hop (Humulus lupulus) are particularly useful as sleeping aids. These herbs can be bought loose and made into a small sleep pillow made from organic cotton. Breathing in the scent of the aromatic herbs as you fall asleep will help you to rest peacefully so you wake refreshed to face the rigours of modern life. Try herb teas as well; limeflower is traditionally supposed to aid sleep, and chamomile is soothing.

151

Make your own household cleaner from less harmful ingredients, which you can buy in large chemists, department stores and hardware shops or even online from eco-suppliers. This is a favourite: mix one teaspoon washing soda, four teaspoons borax and one teaspoon liquid soap or detergent with four cups of hot water in a lidded plastic bottle or old spray container. Shake well to blend and dissolve the minerals. Spray the cleaner onto the surface you're cleaning or apply it with a cloth, wiping it off with a rag as you go. For tougher dirt, leave the mix on for a few minutes before removing. Shake the bottle each time before using. To save time, money and packaging, make your cleaner in advance and buy the ingredients in bulk. Experiment to find a blend that suits you, and maybe add your favourite essential oils or herbs for fragrance.

Sometimes it pays to be a neighbourhood snoop. Next time there is settled snow or frost, take a look at the roof of your home. If the snow or frost there is melting faster than the guy next door's, it's because your loft insulation isn't doing its job. Heat from inside your home is escaping upwards, causing the icy covering to melt. Up to 25 per cent of heat is lost through un-insulated roofs, so having the recommended 11 inches (270mm) of insulation in the loft should help conserve energy, keep your house warmer and result in a drop in your annual fuel bill.

Have a go at making your own herbal oils for the bath. Buy a good quality organic base oil such as olive oil. Decant a little oil into a small bottle and add a few sprigs of your favourite organic herb. If you have herbs such as lavender in the garden, try that for a relaxing, calming bath, and rosemary is great for a stimulating bath to help clarify your thoughts. Pop a couple of sprigs into the oil, screw on the bottle top and leave the bottle in a warm place; after a week, replace the herbs with a fresh sprig. Repeat for three to four weeks for a strongly scented oil. Then add it to your bath water.

154

If you upgrade a piece of technology, pass on your old one. Your out-of-date PC could be a lifeline for schools and community organisations in the developing world. Dedicated charities will take your old hardware, recondition it and send it on to people in need. They can also make use of mice, keyboards, modems, cables and power leads, memory and other peripheral parts. Other items in demand are CD or DVD players/writers, multimedia peripherals, USB devices/cables, multimedia cards and sound cards. Some organisations have a minimum number or specification, while others may like a donation. Get details from your local council, or the manufacturer.

One cost-effective way of finding your way through the alternative energy maze is to bring in a professional eco-consultant or environmental auditor who can give you the lowdown on your individual potential in energy saving. You may have to pay them a fee, but you're sure to get that back and more when your utility bills plummet! An auditor can talk you through the pros and cons of heavy-duty hardware such as wind turbines and ground source pumps, where it's all too easy to get bogged down in information overload.

Make friends with your foes. Some common weeds, such as nettles and dandelions, can be used in cooking or herbal remedies. Try nettle as a herbal tea (you may need to add a little honey to give it some taste), or make the smaller top leaves into a lovely green springtime soup decorated with a swirl of crème fraiche. Use dandelion leaves as a salad ingredient – go for the young ones as the older ones can be bitter – and wash them well.

157

Go online to estimate your carbon footprint. You'll need to know how much gas, electricity or other fossil fuels you've used over a year. If you own a car, you'll need to know the mileage and model. Then think back to your holidays, and any regular commutes you do, to roughly work out your year's worth of travel. When you key this information into the calculator it should convert it into a figure that shows your carbon emissions in tonnes per year – your very own dark mark!

158

Keep tabs on your wardrobe so you don't become a wasteful hoarder. If you haven't worn something for a year, out it should go! But your idea of a designer disaster could be someone else's dress to-die-for, so why not get together with a few friends and host a clothes swap party? If each guest brings along a bag full of wearable but unwanted clothes, chances are between you you'll be able to swap quite a few outfits over a glass of wine or two. Any remaining items can be donated to charity.

159

Instead of buying dubious cheap plastic pet toys made from petrochemicals and probably shipped half way across the world, why not have a go at making your own? A small pine cone makes a great toy for cats. They can throw cones around as they are light, and can be tied on a string for easy batting. A bunch of feathers tied on a cord gives hours of fun – as well as being cheap and natural.

160

There has recently been a resurgence of interest in knitting your own jumpers and other garments. Why not have a go, but use one of the delicious organic fibres available – from merino wool to alpaca, angora, bamboo and hemp? Find out more about what is available (in a myriad of gorgeous colours) at suppliers springing up to meet demand, such as Garthenor Organic New Wool, Myriad, Eweporium Organic Fiber Arts, Shetland Sheep & Angora Rabbitry.

161

If you are a little worried about collecting wild food, grow some on your own patch. Wild strawberries have tiny sweet fruits and can easily be grown from seed. Wild rocket also grows well if you like to gather it in large quantities for salads. Violets and primroses look beautiful and can be crystallised for sweets, which also make attractive gifts.

162

If you live in a town or city, joining a car club is a brilliant way of cutting down on petrol emissions and will save you loads in running costs as well. You only hire the car when you need it, but this can be by the hour, week, month or longer. Membership gives you access to a pool of cars near your home, which you can book in advance or on the day, and covers road tax, insurance, servicing, maintenance and valeting. Most car clubs are run on very simple lines – you can log in online (or by phone) and reserve your car on the spot. A pin number enables you to drive the car away.

163

If insulating your entire home in one go looks too costly, make a start by heat-proofing your favourite rooms, for example the kitchen or the living room. And if double glazing or cavity wall insulation is out of your reach, kick off with cheap measures such as thick curtains or window sealants. To gauge how draughty a room is simply hold up the palm of your hand to the window, floorboards or closed door and feel the change in temperature; if cold air is coming in, warm air is going out! Or hold up a piece of ribbon and watch it flutter…

164

Have you ever thought of keeping a trio of hens in your garden? If you don't keep a rooster, there is no noise to disturb the neighbours. Hens are easy and cheap to keep, and collecting warm eggs is a delight not to be missed. They help to clear pests from the garden, too. Scout about and see if there is an allotment association near you – many of these include hen keepers. They will be only too glad to give you advice and may even be able to sell you a few surplus pullets. Your chicken house can be cheap and home made (there are many patterns online) or top of the range – your hens will be happy in either!

165

If you're not quite wedded to the idea of recycling yet, why not try it for one week? In just seven days you will be astonished (and possibly horrified) to see a small mountain of recyclable newspapers, food packaging, bottles, vegetable peelings and lawn cuttings build up. But recycle and your usual bin-bags will shrink to almost nothing!

166

Have a go at trench composting. It is best started in the autumn to give the waste time to rot, weather and settle before planting in the spring. Dig a trench a spade wide and deep – make it as long as you need. Pile the soil by the trench as you will need it soon. Drop kitchen waste such as peelings into the trench and cover them with a thin layer of soil. This helps the waste to be exposed to a large number of micro-organisms to speed rotting. Alternate layers of waste and soil until the trench is full. This sort of trench is a brilliant place to grow greedy feeders such as runner beans and peas.

6

be arsed...
to sort out
your finances
(hoping for that big lottery win won't cut it)

167

Give yourself pause for thought in the purchasing process - try an experiment along these lines: work out how much you put on your cards last month and draw that sum out in cash. For the next month, try paying for everything with that money. Turning barely noticed credit card spend into extremely visible cash-burn can be quite a shocking way to discover just how much you get through. Alternatively, you may find that using real rather than virtual money inhibits your spending impulses.

168

Build your financial literacy. Generally speaking, we pay very little heed to managing our money unless circumstances force us to. There are plenty of things we can do to rectify this. Try browsing the financial sections of the weekend papers, attending a money management course, or taking up opportunities for annual reviews of your mortgage and bank accounts.

169

The overriding advice for anybody buying just about anything is to avoid as far as possible jumping into the transaction. Realistically, yes, there will be times when you need to move quickly. That bargain in the sales, for example, might require a speedy decision to buy or else risk losing out. But on most occasions, just bear the wisdom of another Latin phrase: festina lente - hurry slowly.

170

If you buy a computer game when it first comes out, it's likely to retail at or around its recommended retail price. Give it six months and often it will be discounted heavily. Likewise, unless you're a fashion slave, hold on for the sales.

171

If you have a savings account, remember to keep an eye on interest rates. One of the very worst things you can do to your finances is to put money away and forget about it. If you open a savings account and take your eye off the interest rate it pays, you often end up being stitched up good and proper.

172

Try haggling for one-off items like paintings, musical instruments or just about anything second-hand. In these cases, there's no fixed value involved and the item is essentially worth whatever the two parties agree it's worth. So, to take a tuba, for example, try telling the seller something along the lines of you like the item but you never pay more than £250 for a tuba, or perhaps that you have a 'strict budget' of £250. You'll be amazed how often you land a real bargain this way.

173

Many businesses that go bust do so not as a result of making a poor major investment decision, but rather on the back of small, almost invisible, but bank-balance sapping expenditures – replacing a printer cartridge, train and taxi fares, telephone bills and so on. In other words, businesses tend to research and monitor the big spends, while the minor sums slip off the financial radar. The same can be true of us individually when it comes to managing personal expenditure.

174

You are storing up problems if you consistently overspend, even if it's only by a small amount. To give an example: your disposable income is £180 a week, but you're spending £200. On that basis, your debt is growing by £1,040 a year – and that's before adding in the interest, probably in the region of 15 per cent a year. It doesn't matter how high your income is if you consistently spend more than you earn.

175

Looking to pay off the mortgage early is a good aspiration but not if you end up struggling to make ends meet. There's no sense saving interest on your mortgage – one of the cheapest ways of borrowing money – only to end up paying higher rates of interest on overdrafts and credit cards that you don't have the financial resources to clear. You can always start overpaying on your mortgage once you have your finances under control. Alternatively, you could direct the overpayment amount into a savings account. This'll give you a reserve fund that you could use if needed.

176

A 2004 survey suggested that abstaining from chocolate, alcohol, coffee, crisps and cigarettes during Lent could net savers around £660. The bank that undertook the survey calculated that giving up a daily latte between Ash Wednesday and Easter can leave savers £86 better off, while foregoing a daily pint of lager could save £92. Smokers who buy a packet of cigarettes a day could save over £200.

177

When it comes to deciding specifically how much money we want to earn to have 'enough', we need to take stock of every aspect of our lives – the home we want, the work we do, the lifestyle we're after, etc. Each of us will have our own answers to these questions, but I'd advise you to be sure that you've taken into account the long term. After all, none of us wants to outlive our money.

178

We all need to keep a more concentrated eye on property prices. We can't simply assume that property prices will continue to rise and that we just need to keep on paying the mortgage and waiting for our eventual property windfall. Whatever the future might hold, we would be wise to recognise the need to more actively monitor and manage our property portfolio.

7

be arsed...
to be a great parent

(no, going to the supermarket on a
Wednesday evening is not a family outing)

179

Involving your child in food shopping and meal preparation will encourage a healthy appetite. Ask her to fill a bag with the best-looking apples she can find at the supermarket for example, or ask her to choose a piece of fish from the fish counter (even if it's 'for daddy' initially). Get her to help you chop the veg with a plastic knife, measure out some rice or lay the table. A little enthusiasm for good, healthy food will go a long way.

180

If your child asks for something special – an electric guitar, hi-fi equipment, an iPod – sit him down and talk about strategies for getting the object of his desire. You may be willing to give him part of the purchase price, perhaps as a birthday present. Then help him to work out how to come up with the rest of the money – saving pocket money, doing extra chores, getting a part time job – and help him to shop around to get the best deal. When he has managed to buy the object of his desires, he's likely to treasure it more because of the effort involved in obtaining it.

181

Home-made lemonade is just the thing for a hot, sunny day. Slice in half then juice 4 lemons (remove any pips as you go). Mix the lemon juice and 100g/3 1/2 oz caster sugar together in a large jug until the sugar is dissolved. Add handfuls of ice to the jug, then 1 litre of sparkling mineral water. Give it all a good stir and serve.

182

When you go out, tell your child where you are going and give him a contact number (or take your mobile phone). Give him an idea of the time you will be back, and if your plans change give him a call. If you model thoughtful behaviour to him – letting the people who love you know where you are and what time you will be back – he is more likely to see its value and treat you in the same way.

183

Why not buy the book of a film your family have enjoyed? By necessity a film can only contain a fraction of the action or plot in a book and this additional material is a great way of extending the pleasure. This often leads on to reading other stories by the same author. Watching *Babe* could prepare your young readers to discover the whole of Dick King Smith's canon.

184

You'll find that if you don't actually ring fence time to spend as a family, it won't happen. It doesn't have to be an 'official' time, as that can get forced. But make sure that every single week, you do something together. Why not cook a meal with your children? Apart from giving you time to talk, it can be great fun. If your children are old enough, make it something that entails lots of chopping, slicing and other time-consuming preparations and it will really create a sense of something achieved together. It may even teach them how to make a few meals!

185

Children often throw wobblies because they are frustrated by all the things they cannot do. Offering choices makes them feel less helpless. If you have decided your son is having soup for lunch, try suggesting a choice: tomato or chicken. Don't ask if he wants soup for lunch unless you are prepared for him to say no.

186

When it comes to your child's health – regular exercise is just as important as a balanced diet. It is recommended that children and young people have at least 60 minutes of exercise every day. It is also recommended that activities that increase muscle strength, flexibility and improve bone strength such as swimming, cycling, sports and dancing should be included at least twice a week.

187

Encourage your children to discover their history. Ask grandparents to photocopy letters, school reports, certificates, photographs and marriage licences. Unlike the originals, it won't matter if little hands leave marks. Next time grandparents visit, they can make a scrapbook with your children, preserving important stories and sharing their cultural and religious traditions. Children can add to this book as they grow older and meet other family members, perhaps interviewing them about their lives, memories, hopes, dreams and regrets. Older children can make videos or recordings of these interviews, and include music from their grandparents' era. Another child can be assigned the role of family librarian, photographing and cataloguing family heirlooms, recording dates of acquisition and potted biographies of previous owners.

188

If you find your daughter's make up application a little heavy handed for daytime use, try to show her the difference between a casual gloss and full 'going out' war paint. Taking turns is great fun – you make up your daughter and let her do your make up. If you are feeling brave, agree to go out for a coffee in your full regalia! Alternatively you could just book a mother-daughter makeover with a makeup artist at a store cosmetic counter as a bonding experience.

189

Try to make at least one 'date' with your teens each week, even if it's just a girly shopping trip or a bite together at a burger bar. If you can't be there when they come home from school, try to eat together as a family round the table at least a couple of times a week for shared time when everyone can catch up.

190

Try changing how you speak to your children. Your aim is to tell them what you want them to do, rather than grumble about what they are doing wrong. So instead of yelling, 'Stop shouting at once', try a comment like, 'Please speak more quietly'. Instead of, 'Will you stop running', say, 'Please walk slowly'. Have a go at turning every complaint into a request for an hour. Your child's response will amaze you.

191

Worried about the additives in ready meals? If you don't feel like cooking every day, by doubling quantities when you do cook and freezing leftovers, the freezer will always be full of home-made ready meals. If raisins, dried fruit like mango strips, seeds and nuts are easily available and there is always fresh fruit like a bowl of shiny plums available, the temptation for crisps or sweets is diminished. That way you can stick to your resolve of making junk food an occasional treat rather than a convenience.

192

Avoid getting into a negative mindset with your teen. Think about how your parents made you feel about yourself when you were a teenager. Visualise yourself back in that situation. This will allow you to contextualise your teen's attitude towards you, and may help you to manage your own behaviour.

193

For fun picnics pack up individual bags of food for children and write their names on them – they'll love delving in to see what's inside. You could even include a cheap gift in each – a styrofoam glider or bottle of bubbles perhaps. Just make sure they're all the same to avoid squabbles.

194

Don't sweat the small stuff. A hyper controlling attitude raises tension within families. It makes kids (and adults) want to rebel. If you turn into a hectoring control freak, fussing over every minor transgression, your child will be more likely to turn into a mini tyrant, and won't develop the independence necessary to function outside the family.

195

If your children interrupt you when you're busy, don't pretend to listen, only giving them half your attention. Instead, say, 'I'm just in the middle of something important, but if you come back in five minutes, I'll have the time to really listen to you.' If you pretend to listen, children soon catch you out and pay you back when it's their turn.

196

Have a go at household haggling. A job children want you to do is contingent on a job they need to do. For example, next time your son asks you to drive him to football training, negotiate. Try saying, 'Yes I'll drive you as soon as you give the guinea-pig some food and water.' Avoid nagging or reminding, and stick to your agreement. If he dawdles and is late for football training, he's learnt an important lesson about responsibility.

197

Kids will love growing their own beansprouts. Get hold of some mung beans – rinse, then soak in clean water for 12 hours. Rinse again, and pour the beans into a clean glass container. Cover the container with clingfilm to stop the beans drying out – and place on a cool, bright window ledge. Rinse the beans and replace in the container every morning and every evening (this is important to avoid mould formation). Within 4–5 days your beans should have started to germinate. Your crop is ready to eat when most of your sprouts have developed two small leaves.

198

Invite your child to talk on a subject they feel particularly strongly about. Maybe there is an issue between you and your daughter over why she must go to bed at a certain time? Let her talk for two minutes without interruption and then it's your go. It will teach her the skill of listening and appreciating the views of others.

199

During a family meal why not get everyone to brainstorm a difficult homework question? It could open all sorts of new avenues and make what otherwise might have been a hard slog into an assignment your son or daughter will enjoy.

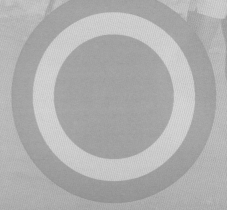

200

If your teenager is defiant and rude to you, take a deep breath and calmly explain to him that you would not accept this behaviour from another adult. Tell him that if he insists on talking to you in this way you will not listen – you would ignore a persistently abusive adult. It may initially make him angry, but he needs to learn the lesson that this behaviour is unacceptable, even in adults. If you shout and yell back, you are validating his behaviour with attention. Stop it dead in its tracks and be prepared to persist with this strategy: it is hard to do, but it works.

201

Look for opportunities to ask your child's advice. Whether she's helping to program your new mobile phone, picking a shirt and tie for you to wear to work or helping you decide what the family should eat for dinner, involving them in decisions helps them feel they have an important contribution to make and that you trust them.

202

If you are finding your teen unlovable, think about the time before the problems started. Use videos of family occasions, photos of birthday parties, holidays and trips as props. Hold on to the warm, loving feelings these memories awaken. When you look at your stroppy teen, remember the child he once was and visualise the great adult he will one day be, and it will help you to cope with the difficulties of the 'here and now'.

203

In warm weather – make your own fruit lollies. Lolly moulds can be bought cheaply from most major department stores and large supermarkets. Fill the moulds with fruit juice or fresh fruit puree (strawberries, raspberries, kiwis and pineapple all work well) and freeze for two hours. Experiment with exotic fruit cocktails or blend fruit with vanilla yogurt or banana for smoothies-on-a-stick. Stripy lollies look great too. Use two or three different fruit purees – allowing each layer to freeze for an hour before you add the next.

204

Encourage your child to be constructive in his criticism by getting him to elaborate on his answers. After a family day out sit down with him and produce an objective critique of what went on. What were the good and bad points of the day and why? What could have been more fun and what would he have done differently if he'd been in charge of organising everything?

205

Next time you go out, get your children to choose a suitable place to cross the road and tell you when it's safe to cross. As soon as they can try new ideas out in practice, they'll be reinforced and remembered. Or ask a question like, 'Say you got lost here, who could you ask for help?' Try to keep your tone casual, or you'll frighten them, and they'll be clingy rather than independent.

206

If your child is old enough to shape Plasticine or Play Doh, she can make petits fours for your next dinner party. Colour marzipan with a few drops of food colouring. Kids like to do the next bit: knead the colour into the marzipan until it is evenly coloured. With orange, yellow, green and red marzipan, they'll be able to make a selection of fruit and veg, moulding little spheres of marzipan as if it was any other modelling material. Use cloves to make stalks on apples and pears and push them right in to make the bottom of an orange. They look stunning in petit four cases. If you don't have a party planned, they can be made in advance and stored in a box with layers of tissue paper between them. Your child might also like to make animals to decorate an iced cake for a special occasion.

207

Avoid arguments about chores by offering choices instead of giving instructions. Instead of saying, "Wash the dishes," say "Are you going to wash the dishes as soon as we finish dinner or after we watch the film?" This gives your teenager some control over the chore and she is less likely to feel hemmed in and complain. Note, however, you are taking it as a given that she will wash the dishes. If your teenager says she doesn't want to do either, smile and tell her that wasn't one of the choices and repeat the options.

208

When you are talking to your child, divorce behaviour from 'self'. That means you criticise the behaviour you find unacceptable, rather than your child – and that avoids labelling him. For example, if your child leaves the bathroom looking like a swamp, don't call him a slob; tell him he needs to pick up after himself instead of expecting other people to do it.

209

If visits to large supermarkets are stressing you and the kids out, why not make shorter and more frequent visits to local shops? Specialist butchers, bakers, organic greengrocers and sweet shops are being steamrollered by the big boys and it might be the only chance your kids have to see small community stores in action. Older children can go on errands to learn independence. Give your son a list of few items you need and give him enough money to cover it. He'll learn to find items, queue at a till, pay, count change and check it against the receipt.

210

If there is a big family birthday approaching ask your child to compose a special poem for that person. It could be funny or heartfelt and included with a birthday card. If he is feeling really brave he could give a rendition of the poem at the party. This is not about creating the best poem in the world but seeing the recipient chuffed to bits and your child receiving lots of praise for his efforts.

211

Put a basket or plastic box for each family member in the cupboard under the stairs or any other hidden but accessible place. When you find 'stuff' cluttering rooms, dump it in the appropriate box. Then pick a time, perhaps at the weekend, when boxes are expected to be emptied and things put away. If you are tight for space, use one big glory box and people can rummage for their stuff – if they don't like it, they should put their stuff away. Be prepared to take a hard line with your teen; tell him it goes in a bin bag if it is not put away by the deadline, because he obviously does not value the item.

212

Be a healthy role model. If you are constantly on a diet, you are setting your growing child a bad example. She will learn that her weight is something to obsess about. Likewise, if you make jokes about your teen being chubby, you are giving her the message that thinner is better. Avoid making comments about body size – yours, hers, or anyone else's for that matter.

213

The next time your child is going on a trip without you, make them prepare early to grow in confidence. What clothes or cuddly toys will they take? You can sprinkle some magic 'make me brave' fairy dust over everything. Why not get your child to write a thank-you letter in advance. As much as possible let your child make her own plans so she feels independent and mentally prepared to fly solo.

214

While the weather's horrible, why not catch up with some housework? Children will help, especially if you involve young kids in a new game: sorting laundry. Toddlers are able to sort all the socks into one pile, while older children can do something more ambitious like folding. This teaches children how to put things into categories, which is the basis of science.

215

It is virtually inevitable that your teen will drink alcohol at some point, so teach her to drink responsibly. Teach her to 'pace' herself, alternating alcoholic drinks with mineral water or juice. Advise her to have a starchy meal such as pasta before going to a party and tell her never to drink on an empty stomach. Encourage her to plan what she would do if she found herself in a dangerous situation due to drink – to look out for friends who may be drunk and to ring home if she gets into difficulties.

216

Make sure you make time to give your child full attention when he or she is talking to you. Stop what you are doing and look at your child's face. Do not just carry on with whatever task you are doing. Turn towards her and be an 'active' listener – actually engage with what she says. This gives your child the message that what she says – and by implication, she herself – is important to you.

217

Take children to a local pick-your-own farm. Kids will really enjoy a Sunday afternoon spent picking – and, of course, eating – strawberries, raspberries or blackberries. Alternatively, get your child to grow her own fruit – even if you don't have a garden. Strawberries and tomatoes (yes, the latter are, of course, fruit) do really well in pots, window boxes and gro-bags and are easy to look after. You can buy starter plants very cheaply from all garden centres at the beginning of the summer.

218

Make sure your teen knows that you do not subscribe to the negative view of teenagers promoted in the media. Discuss the issues raised in media reports with your child, and keep channels of communication open. Make sure they 'overhear' you praising actions taken by young people in society. Do not let a 'them and us' culture develop in your family.

219

Fun or unusual shaped pasta is a really worthwhile investment when it comes to getting your child interested in a meal. Whilst most supermarkets offer a wide selection of pasta, the more unusual child-friendly shapes and baby pastas can sometimes be hard to find. If you're passing – always be sure to check the selections in Italian delis and upmarket food halls, and if you're on holiday in Europe, the local supermarket is always worth a quick look. If you find a shape you think your kids will love – stock up, buying at least one more bag than you think you'll need.

220

Give your child and her friends a disposable or digital camera to make a photo story with speech bubbles. Keep the story short, with maybe five pictures. Make sure they write a brief script and everyone plays a character they are happy with. The children can make costumes and construct the set. They can add the speech bubbles to the pictures later or use computer technology to create a magazine photo story.

221

If you have rules, you need sanctions for when the rules are broken. Reasonable consequences should ideally be tied in to the infraction i.e. using the phone repeatedly for chats during peak cost tariff time, despite being asked not to could lead to not being able to use the telephone for a period. Not calling home to let you know he is going to be later than expected could lead to not being allowed out the next weekend etc.

222

The better informed you are about drugs and their effects the more credibility your teenager will give your views. Find out about the effects of drugs on the Internet, or by picking up a booklet at your local health centre.

8

be arsed...
to challenge your brain
(there's more to learn than this week's celebrity diet secrets)

223

Improve your ability to think on the hoof by join a debating society, a book club or any forum where you have to exchange views in 'real time'. If you can track one down in your neck of the woods, consider signing up for a stand-up comedy workshop.

224

If you have trouble remembering people's names, try using a handy memory prompt. For example, associate the person's name with an animal whose name begins with the same letter for example antelope for Alice. Visualise distinguishing characteristics such as a moustache, funky glasses or long black hair so you can use them as prompts at a later date. It also helps to remember their name if you repeat it aloud when first introduced and use it several times during the course of your first conversation.

225

Looking for a new hobby? Take up tango dancing – scientists have specifically identified it as an activity which reduces the risk of developing Alzheimer's by an astonishing 75%. It seems this activity demands an unusual combination of multi-tasking, mixing mental and physical activities, thereby helping to maintain a robust hippocampus.

226

Be aware that we all have different strengths in learning new information. Some people prefer to study by listening, others by reading, writing, hearing themselves speak or doing (such as building models or operating a piece of equipment). By becoming aware of your preferred method(s) of learning, you can choose to learn more in that way.

227

Consider signing up for a part-time class at a local college. Don't let any bad memories of school classrooms put you off; most adult evening classes are far more informal and fun. Plus you get to choose what you want to study. Who knows, not only will it stimulate your mind, but it could give your career a boost. Think about what subjects you always wanted to study, but perhaps felt were too frivolous or complicated.

228

Learn to speed read. It's a useful skill that also improves mental alertness. Practise with a newspaper. Scan through the story to get an idea of content and context. Next, move your fingertip across the page underlining the words as you read. This anchors your eyes and frees you from having to repeat every word inside your head. Soon you'll be able to skip to every third line and eventually get the gist from just a few lines on any page. It works to make your brain patterns more alert and zippy.

229

Test and strengthen your ability to recall buildings and places. Think of how many buildings you can recall in detail. These can include previous homes, homes of friends or relatives, schools or shopping malls. Take a few minutes when you won't be disturbed, close your eyes and visualise walking through the building. The more you do this, the more you will strengthen your ability to visually recall buildings and places.

230

Try your hand at drawing. It's a great way to increase your ability to visualise. Even if you think you're bad at drawing, you can soon improve through practice. Anyway, the aim is not to become the next Da Vinci, but to increase your awareness of your visual sense. Start by placing an object in front of you, look at it and absorb as many details as you can. Then look away and try to sketch it. Then look back and compare your sketch with the object; note any details you missed.

231

Ever heard the phrase 'fake it till you make it'? Often simply acting as though you were in a particular state of mind can help you get into that state. This is true of concentrated attention. Boost your attentiveness towards something by adopting the posture and facial expressions you would be using if you were naturally fascinated by it. Sit or stand upright or even lean slightly forward, and keep your eyes open wide.

232

Keep a notepad with you at all times; you never know when you might need to jot down important information. A small pad that fits easily into a pocket is best. Most of the time, for most people, paper is still better than electronic organisers, as it's quicker to use, and you don't need to be so worried about it being stolen. Important long-term notes can then be transferred to a digital storage medium later.

233

If you're learning a language, try listening to a radio station in the language you are learning. Many radio stations can now be accessed online. By listening regularly you will be subconsciously absorbing the language in its everyday form. Vocabulary, rhythm and pronunciations will become more familiar to you. Vocabulary and pronunciation that you had been explicitly trying to learn will be repeated, meaning they are more likely to be encoded into your long-term memory.

234

Try memorising a short poem. Read it through several times at bedtime, attempt to recite it without looking a couple of times, check where you want wrong and then sleep on it. In the morning, with just one quick read-through, try and recite the whole thing again over your cornflakes. Chances are you'll be nigh-on perfect. Within weeks, you too could become a walking fount of poetry. (You may find yourself breakfasting alone, though…)

235

Take a selection of emails, letters and reports you've received recently. Read them through and then jot down what you think the core message is in each case. As well as improving your summarising skills, it will help you to focus your thinking on the key messages in your own communications.

236

Think of an area you are skilled in that you would like to progress far further in. Make a list of problems in that field that you're uncertain of being able to crack, and resolve to solve them! Join organisations and groups in that field for whom you only just qualify. Spend time with people who are slightly more skilled than you in the area you are trying to master.

237

The next time you are in your car use familiar landmarks (pubs, buildings, road junctions and so on) to create a story. The purpose of this is to get you confident in the application of the concept before you apply it to memorising important things, so your story can be anything you like. Once you have finished your journey, try and remember the landmarks and the story together. After a couple of days, repeat the journey and see if the landmarks bring the story back to life. If it works, then give it a try with your study material.

238

Trying to learn a new musical instrument? Make an audio recording of yourself just playing randomly on the instrument, then listen to it straight away. Then repeat. This creates a feedback loop that can accelerate your mastery of the instrument. The same principle was tried with babies learning to talk (their babbles were recorded and played back instantly to them), which seemed to rapidly accelerate their language development.

239

Try explaining whatever it is you're trying to learn to someone else. The very act of having to explain it will force you to make sure you understand it clearly. Also, the act of explaining it in your own words will help you to restructure the information in a way that makes most sense to you. Try explaining it out loud to a person, then try explaining it in writing to someone else. Finally, try explaining it in such simple language that a twelve-year-old child could grasp it.

240

A good tool for capturing your stream-of-consciousness thoughts and ideas is to get into the habit of journaling. Buy a notebook and every morning – preferably as soon as you get up – set aside 20–30 minutes to write two or three pages of anything that comes to mind. This could be problems you encountered the day before, ideas, dreams, rambling thoughts and so on. It's a curious experience. Initially, you'll find yourself writing about fairly trivial stuff ('feeling a bit crap today', 'it's raining', 'think I'll have muesli for breakfast'), but you can quickly find yourself exploring some fairly deep terrain.

241

Flashcards – blank postcard-sized cards which you can write and draw on – are a great way to summarise information you are trying to learn. Not only will the process of writing out the information help you memorise it, but so will the process of simplifying it in order to fit it on the card. If you find it hard to simplify the information, try breaking it down onto multiple cards, or try repeatedly writing out the information with fewer words, until only a small number of words trigger it all.

242

Productivity experts recommend that you make your to-do items as specific as possible. Rather than just list one – for example, such as 'contact Bill' – specify how you will contact him: 'phone Bill' or 'email Bill'. Take as many of the decisions about a task at the beginning when you are writing them down, and you will make it easier to complete your to-do list, as less decision making will be needed to get through it.

243

If you've got the time and willpower, large amounts of text can be memorised by the sheer force of repetition. Start off by reading the first one or two sentences, then look away or close your eyes and try and repeat them. Look back to the text and see how accurate you were. If you were unable to repeat the sentences, read them again, then try again until you can. Then add a couple more sentences in and try to repeat them all. Continue this process, accumulating longer and longer stretches of text in your memory.

244

Keep an eye out for games that will help you to practise holding lots of information in your mind at once. There are many card and video games which require players to memorise a number of pieces of information. These will enable you to increase the volume of information you can hold at once in your working memory, whilst also having fun.

245

If you're studying, take a little time out and go somewhere quiet and away from distraction. Think about the following questions: What do you like about studying? What do you dislike about studying? What could you do to make the process of studying more enjoyable? What sort of environment do you need to make your study more productive? What resources could you utilise to make your study more effective? By answering these questions honestly, you'll have the basis for understanding your attitude to study and what you can do to make it a better experience for you.

246

Borrow a complicated piece of kit from a neighbour or friend – a hedge cutter, say, or a concrete mixer – and try and work out under your own steam how to become, if not expert, then at least adequate at trimming hedges or mixing concrete. This isn't just a boy thing, by the way – it's just as important for creative women to challenge themselves and the people around them by working with kit like this.

247

Improve concentration. Stick on some Mozart. Research from the University of California shows that people who listened to the Sonata for Two Pianos in D Major while preparing for an IQ test scored higher than those who studied in silence. Mozart is the gold standard but any rhythmic music will help as long as it doesn't have lyrics which disrupt concentration.

248

Why not write about things you love thinking about? Things you've experienced in the past and believe other people will be interested in. This really is living in the moment – you'll have to give total concentration to the craft of writing and you'll become lost in the task.

249

If you can't remember a name, try running through the alphabet, starting by asking yourself 'Does it begin with "a"?' and so on. This method might seem longwinded, but you should be able to move through the alphabet within a few minutes, and it typically takes more than a few minutes to otherwise remember a name which is on the tip of your tongue. Once you've found the letter that it begins with, this is often enough to trigger the memory of the word.

250

Learn to think like an author you admire. Physically copy out (preferably by hand, although you could type) a page of text by an author whose thinking you admire. Do this several times and you may start to absorb subconsciously their style and way of structuring information.

251

Are you trying to learn a complex physical skill, like driving, touch-typing or a particular sport? Simply break the skill down into parts and master each part, before bringing them together as a whole. Take magicians, for example. They will practise particular hand movements repetitively for hours so that they can perform them smoothly, and without having to think, when they need to do so in their shows.

252

If you're giving a speech and have it written out in full, first turn each sentence into a couple of 'prompt words' which will trigger the whole sentence or paragraph. Write out your prompt words, then test whether you can remember the whole speech just by looking at them. Once you've managed that, transfer your prompt words to a set of cards, which you can use as a backup in your presentation. A brief glance at each card should be enough to trigger at least a paragraph's worth of your speech.

253

Try an experiment to establish your optimum study time. Over the course of a week study at specific times and assess your levels of alertness and effectiveness. So on Monday, you might get up at 06:00 and study until 10:00 am. On Tuesday you could get up at 09:00 and study between 12:00 and 16:00. On another day you could have a longer lie in, busy yourself during the day and get down to study at 19:00 and work through until 23:00. When recording your levels of alertness and effectiveness, note how awake you feel, how focused you are and how productive you are. It shouldn't be long before you have sussed out what time is best for you.

254

Try keeping a dream diary in order to get into the habit of remembering your dreams. Simply keep a notebook and pencil next to your bed, and when you wake up in the morning – or even in the middle of the night – and can remember what you had been dreaming about, jot down as many details as possible. All new memories quickly fade away if we don't think about them, and particularly memories of our dreams. This means you should jot down your dreams quickly as soon as you wake.

255

A party can be a great opportunity to practise remembering names. At the end of the party – assuming you aren't drunk – try and recall the names of all the new people you met. Then try and recall them again the following morning. Remember, the best way to burn a name into your memory is to repeat it upon meeting the person, and try and build an association between their name and the way they look.

256

When learning a new language, remember that even though it has a huge vocabulary, usually only a minority of words form the majority of the words in regular use. Research which words are the most heavily used in order to focus your memorising where it will have the most effect.

257

Try remembering one poem per week. Each evening, before you go to bed, repeat the poem several times. Start by learning the first verse, then the second, and so on. Then, each week, test yourself on the whole poem from the previous week. Remember that the rhythm and rhyme within most poems will be a natural memory aid.

258

Create and memorise a map of your own past. Although you are unlikely to ever sit an examination testing you on which year various events occurred in your life, it can be enormously helpful to remember what you did each year. Get a notebook and write down each year of your life so far. Then, next to each year, try to write several key events. The more time you spend on this, the more likely you will continue to remember more and more events you thought were long forgotten.

259

Strengthen your conscious awareness of scents. Take a moment to smell the air wherever you are now. Is the odour pleasant, neutral or unpleasant? Do this each time you enter a new environment.

be arsed...
to nurture the inner you
(it's time to get touchy-feely,
and it's not just for girls)

260

Promise yourself every day that you'll savour small (free) pleasures. For instance, take off your shoes and walk on damp grass, admire an exhilarating view, rub something delicious on your hands or listen to some uplifting music. Absorb the sensation and allow the pleasure to flow through your body.

261

Do you know who you are? Are you so busy being what your employer, children or partner want you to be that you've lost sight of who you are and what you want from life? Ask yourself this really simple question and write down the answers that first spring to mind. What do I really want from life? Then ask yourself this. If you knew that it is OK for you to do what you want in your life, how might you go about it? This will help you to identify things that you can do whilst acknowledging all the other aspects of your life that you need to consider.

262

Buy a pot of lemon balm and keep it on a sunny windowsill. Crush a leaf and smell that warm, uplifting, citrussy fragrance. Lemon balm has a centuries-old reputation as a feel-good mood-lifter for when you're feeling cold, down and miserable: 'powerfully chasing away melancholy', as one seventeenth-century writer put it. Put a small handful of leaves in a mug, fill with boiling water and steep, covered, for ten minutes. Drink this three times a day.

263

Get two large bowls and fill one with ice-cold water and the other with bath-temperature hot water. Place both feet in the hot water for two minutes, then in the cold water for two minutes. Repeat five times so you're in both hot and cold for a total of ten minutes. It's both invigorating and deliciously relaxing.

264

Book out an entire day to do exactly what you want (within the boundaries of the law, obviously). Plan your day meticulously, as if you're doing it for someone else. What would you like to do? Go to an art gallery? Check into a health spa for the day? Go to the zoo? Have a long bath then go to bed with a good book? Make space for yourself in your life. You need this space to be yourself, to be creative, to be regenerated. Don't feel guilty about it. Enjoy!

265

Set aside time for a regular side-splitting laugh where you rent a funny movie or invite your most amusing friends round for the evening. Giggling helps trigger the production of dopamine, which induces euphoria by stimulating the same part of the brain as drugs such as cocaine!

266

Try saying no in all kinds of situations and see how it feels. Asked to do overtime you don't want to do or babysit a friend's kids? Say no with a smile and don't be tempted to explain – it's a favour they are requiring, not something you have to justify not doing. Be prepared for people to be angry or unreasonable, but remind yourself that those are their emotions and not yours. Once you get into the swing of drawing up boundaries you'll find it easier to stand your ground.

267

Boost your health in five seconds – stroke a cat or pat a dog. Time spent stroking and talking to animals increases endorphins, the feel-good chemicals in the brain, and decreases cortisone, the stress hormone that damages the immune system. If you spend a lot of time alone, it could be worth considering getting a pet – or volunteering to help look after someone else's.

268

Designate Saturday 'family' day and Sunday afternoon 'selfish' time. We can usually find an hour or so on Sunday afternoon to spend on ourselves – just don't let it get filled with chores or your partner's agenda.

269

Right here, right now, turn on a favourite song and sing, dance, or play air-guitar to it. Alternatively leave the radio on and whenever a song that you really enjoy comes on take time out to sing or dance along. This is the perfect time for a break. Most songs are no longer the three or four minutes so it's not as though you will be wasting time. Do this and you'll be more focussed, relaxed, and happy.

270

Set aside an hour and find a pen, some paper and a quiet place. Now imagine the best six months of your life. Not six months that you've already lived or the next six months, but six months of your dreams. Picture yourself at the age of ninety-five telling your great-grandchildren about this incredible six months that you're living, what you're achieving, how happy you are, what a fantastic job you're in, what wonderful relationships you're enjoying, what a beautiful house you're living in, and so on. Describe all this in as much detail as possible. Now put this somewhere that you can see it every day, read it each morning and see what happens. Even better, each day ask yourself, 'If I knew that there is one thing that I can do today that will move me closer to my vision what might that be?' Then do it!

271

Try a comforting bedtime bath. Add 10–15 drops of good essential oil – such as lavender, orange blossom (aka neroli) or the sweet and exotic ylangylang – to the bath water. These aren't just great smells: they are absorbed into the bloodstream through the skin in a matter of minutes to travel the body and work their calming, soothing effect where needed. Relax in this lovely bath for twenty minutes then go straight to bed. Be careful not to apply these oils undiluted to your skin: a good way to disperse them through the bath water is to add them to a cupful of whole milk first and pour them in together.

272

Brighten up your world. Colour experts say orange can be a great pick-me-up so a bowl of oranges on your desk or a vase of marigolds on the sitting-room table will perk you up in no time.

273

Spend the next hour thinking only about the present. Become aware of what you're doing in each moment. Appreciate each moment and become aware of everything in and around you – every movement you make, how your body feels, each sound around you. See how much you can notice while you're doing whatever it is you're doing. Become aware of your breathing and how you're feeling. You may even choose to ask, 'What could I do in this moment, right now, that may improve my life or the life of someone I care about?' The following day you could increase the hour to two hours, then continue to build on this until you start to really live your life in the present moment.

274

Tense shoulders? Sore back? Try an aromatherapy bath. Add a few drops of Scotch pine, which is warming and good for sore muscles, or clary sage, which has anti-inflammatory properties.

275

Thinking happy thoughts boosts the immune system, stressful thoughts can lower levels of immune antibodies. Whenever you feel stressed, close your eyes, take five deep, slow breaths and recall a happy memory. Stay focused on it for five minutes and open your eyes again.

276

Stiff neck, a spot of back pain, achy calf-muscles from overdoing the aerobics? Try ginger, a powerful anti-inflammatory which speeds up the local circulation to relieve pain or swelling. Try a ginger bath: add 2–3 teaspoons of powdered ginger to a pint of hot water and simmer till it turns yellow. Then add it to your bedtime bath.

277

Use your work diary to identify which part of your job you really like, and see if you can do more of this and less of the other stuff. Why not? It's just as easy to make a several changes at one time as it is to make one.

278

Clothes can play a huge part in improving the quality of our lives. Every morning choose one thing that makes your heart sing – a colour you love, a fabric that embraces you, a piece of jewellery with sentimental attachment. Next time you're shopping buy clothes that help you radiate confidence.

279

Make a list of the activities you used to love when you were around 17 or 18 – a pretty sure sign of what the 'real you' really loves. You're looking for a minimum of 10 activities. Pick one and carve out the time to do it in the next week. Work your way through the list of activities that still appeal.

280

Make your own pick-me-up CD or tape. Pick your favourite energising and uplifting pieces of music and play them in the car, as you walk in the park or before that scary meeting. Instant joy!

281

Stimulate acupressure points on your feet. Stiff neck? Gently walking your thumb and fingers across the ball of your foot below your toes then around the base of your big toe. Aching back? Slowly walk your thumb down the inner edge of your foot following the bones along the arch.

282

Look at the people who make you feel good and consider which of their qualities you like. Maybe your grandmother is a very calming person to be around because she is a great listener. Maybe your best friend is brilliant at coming up with exciting plans and making things happen. Your brother might always know how to put nervous people at ease… think about how you can adopt these easy ways of being, and look for similar traits in yourself.

283

Take time to live in your body, rather than using it merely as a tool. Sit on the ground and make yourself comfortable. Push your fingers into the soil and feel its texture. Close your eyes and listen to the sounds you hear, then let them slip away. Breathe deeply, feeling the air filling your lungs. Visualise light and warmth filling your body with every intake of breath; picture murky fragments of tension and stress pouring out as you exhale. Feel the warmth of the sun on your face and the crumbly earth between your fingers before coming slowly back to yourself.

284

Get a sheet of paper and list your reasons to be happy. Start with today's events then cover life in general. Write down anything at all that puts a smile on your face or a warm glow in your belly such as a fantastic family, a great job or even a bargain pair of shoes.

285

Try an aromatherapy upper. Bergamot is said to increase self-esteem and grapefruit can be refreshing and revitalising. Try wallowing in an aromatherapy-infused bath before you head out or pop a few drops on a tissue and inhale deeply two or three times en route to the event.

286

Invest in some special bath props that you keep purely for restoration. The sense of 'specialness' helps turn a bath into an event and with time you will be able to trigger relaxation with just part of the ritual. A cup of tea, a bath with balancing oil or body brushing will in themselves be almost as good as the whole ritual.

287

Think of a game you enjoyed playing as a child, be it Scrabble or Monopoly or even hopscotch. Then… yes, you've guessed it… have a go! Rope in a playmate and enjoy a trip back to childhood. You'll be surprised at how much fun a game you haven't played since childhood can be. It'll rejuvenate you more than any wrinkle cream.

288

Make your morning shower a mini-meditation session through the power of mindfulness. Listen to the sound of the water, and the sensation of the water on your skin. Let thoughts float down the plughole, concentrate only on what your body can feel, see and hear.

289

Dwelling on past hurts will make you feel bitter and resentful, so savour your positive past. Every day for a whole week, set aside five minutes each morning and night to think about some of the loveliest things you've experienced. Research has shown that being positive helps you recover from psychological problems and emerge much stronger. It's also important to remember even though you can't control your past, you can determine your future. Take a pen and paper and imagine who and where you want to be, then work out what steps you need to take.

290

Listen to some Bach, Chopin or Beethoven prior to falling asleep. It's been shown that people who listen to classical music in bed fall asleep more easily and sleep better than people who watch TV or listen to other sorts of music.

291

Go for a traditional cream tea or to an ice cream parlour and enjoy a big treat. If you can't afford that, make your own sundae at home. Ensure you get as many toppings as possible and relish every bite. You are banned from making comments like 'the diet starts tomorrow' or 'this'll go straight to my hips'.

292

Channel your future self. This is an exercise you can do simply for fun. Relax your body and close your eyes for a minute, imagine that you're about 65 years old and about to retire (if you are that age then take it another 20 years forward). Then write down some questions about your life that you'd like answered by your future self. A typical question might be 'Did I live abroad at all?' and then try to see your future self answering that question for you. You don't have to put much store by it but it does open you up to the way you would like things to pan out.

293

Make a compilation CD or download tracks for a personalised mood-busting playlist. That way, whether you're into Motown or mountain dulcimer, you'll always have music to move you when you need a boost.

294

Write out a favourite affirmation on a small slip of paper and slip it into your bra (gentleman, try a pocket rather than anything unhygienic). Then each time you have a loo break during your working day, slip out the affirmation and whisper it to yourself. You can say it completely silently if you're scared someone from accounting might overhear and get the wrong idea.

295

Right before you go to bed, make a wish list. During the day we are so busy with work lists that we forget that you can use the power of the list to manifest lovely, fun things too. Choose something enjoyable like beach holidays or books or restaurants you'd like to visit and make a list of the top ten you'd really like to have or do. Then when each happens, cross it off your list. When the last is done, make a new list!

296

If you're a particularly social person, try a month of accepting no invitations. No parties, cinema trips, dinners or sports dates. And don't invite anyone to yours either. A whole month of abstinence will make you realise how much leisure time you actually have and you can then use it wisely after your month's fast to choose just those activities that truly make you happy rather than those you do out of a sense of obligation.

297

To banish stress related headaches and insomnia, try hand reflexology. Stretch out your right hand and, with your left thumb, apply pressure from the base of your hand and work your way u p to the top of your thumb tip. Repeat ten times. Alternatively, use scent to improve your mood. Drip a few drops of some of the following aromatherapy oils on a tissue to sniff when you feel stress levels rising: jasmine, neroli, lavender, chamomile, vetiver or clary sage.

298

When you're feeling stressed and under attack, mechanical repetitive tasks are good for centring you. Cooking works well; so does weeding the garden. Concentrate fully on your actions. Switch off your brain.

299

Get tucked in. Ask a family member to tuck in your duvet around your bed so you're tightly in there and try relaxing in that position, in the dark, for a time. Only do it for as long as you feel comfortable. You could also play some calming sounds like ocean waves while you're doing this.

300

House sit or house swap with a friend. As the holiday season comes upon us many of our friends who live by the coast or in the city (if we're coastal dwellers) are off on holiday, leaving their homes empty. Ask if they want a house sitter and enjoy an almost free holiday. You'll be shopping for groceries in a new town, discovering new walks and maybe even looking after a dog (a pleasant experience if you're not allowed them in your city flat).

301

Sign up for a regular gym class, running group or swimming night. Setting, and paying for, a routine makes it much harder to put off exercising and gives you a weekly adrenaline injection. You know it makes sense.

302

Today find a recipe that you've never tried before (it can be a very simple assembling one if you're a hopeless cook) and make it tonight. Better still, invent something of your own. A distinct and fabulous cuisine called 'Indo-Chinese' developed when Indian and Chinese chefs in North India took the techniques and ingredients of Chinese cooking and combined them with Indian spicing so don't be afraid of adding your own touch.

303

Get a day pass for a seriously good library that covers the subjects you're especially interested in. Treat it like an outing and read not for work or study but for pleasure, surfing the books like you do the internet. Find the library considered best for your own interests and immerse yourself in knowledge.

304

Perk yourself up with a pedicure. Relaxing foot massages can nurture, cleanse, energise and relax your body and mind.

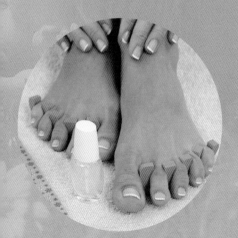

305

This week visit a holy place at an awkward time when no-one is likely to be there. Go in between services to a church or visit a temple at about 9.30 when the early morning worshippers will have gone. You don't need to know what to do, just sit and relax, watching your breath coming in and going out. If religious holy places make you nervous, try visiting a beautiful natural spot or a building you think is architecturally gorgeous.

306

Combine some of mood-enhancing foods and create a delicious gourmet treat, like wholemeal pasta with tuna, cheese and pine nuts, to make your mouth water and mood soar.

307

Save up and visit a spa. A pampering visit to a place that smells nice and is geared toward your relaxation and enjoyment makes you feel like a million pounds sterling. If a spa isn't your scene then perhaps a round of golf somewhere? The point is that if you save up you can sometimes enjoy the same pleasures as the very rich and that will make you realise that the experience and not the bank balance is what really matters.

308

Spend ten minutes today doing something you used to really enjoy. It might be returning to a favourite book, playing a much-loved album or soaking in the tub.

309

To get into a sensual mood, lie back and relax in a warm bath before going to bed. Unwind and imagine tensions and strains washing away. Pamper yourself with soothing bath lotions and sweet-smelling massage oils. If you treat yourself like an Adonis or sex goddess, you'll feel like one.

310

Unhappy with your work life balance? Work out if the advantages of your job are worth the trade off. Make a list of your values and priorities. Then cross off the items on your list that are not really all that important to you. Once you're down to two or three important values, you can see whether your lifestyle and your life fit with those values. If one of your priorities is to see your children and your work makes this impossible, then maybe you should change your lifestyle and schedule. Think about changing shifts. If that's not possible consider another job, retraining or going part time.

311

Try to make your good holiday mood last longer than your tan. Did you enjoy a dip in the ocean? Then try to go to your local pool a couple of times a week: close your eyes and pretend you're back in the Med for a few minutes.

be arsed...
to be a great lover
(there's more to it than sex)

312

Write a letter to the woman or man in your life and leave it for them when they come back from work or the shops. Hide love notes in his suit pocket. Tuck them under her pillow or pop them in her workbag.

313

This evening, turn your dining area into a five-star restaurant. Prepare a handwritten menu of your partner's favourite dishes, put her kind of music on in the background, and cook as much as possible beforehand so you're not tied to the kitchen. Do something special in between courses. Play piano, read her a poem, look into her eyes and tell her what you see.

314

Sexy dates aren't confined to those on first dates. If you've been together for a while then try something really radical like an evening class. You could do tango dancing or art or learn a language together. Seeing each other master a new skill is very sexy.

315

Time for a little live experiment. Spend a day noticing and appreciating all your partner's mini heroics. Try to make at least twelve comments, like: 'I love the way that even though you've been up half the night with the baby, you still look gorgeous.' At the end of the day, spend a little time alone evaluating your partner's responses. You'll probably be pleasantly surprised.

316

Share a bath with your partner tonight. Fluff up some towels in the tumble dryer, fill your bathroom with candles and chill your best bottle of white. Add a few drops of musk-scented oils to the bathwater if you like, but leave your lavender bath salts on the windowsill. Mr Right doesn't want to go to work smelling like someone's granny.

317

Set aside at least fifteen minutes and have a no-tongues kissing session that doesn't lead anywhere else. Rub your lips together, kiss the corners of her mouth to make your partner smile and enjoy all the new and forgotten sensations.

318

Explore every room in your home for new sexy possibilities and think how a simple prop may transform a room into a sex den. Invest in a sheepskin rug for in front of your fire and suddenly you're transported to your own romantic log cabin. A dozen candles to light your bathroom will turn it into a sensual spa. The possibilities are endless.

319

Hammocks are a great place to hang out in, but for the ultimate sensual seat, you need a camomile bed. It's easy to grow one by planting camomile in a low raised bed made with railway sleepers. Fill your bed with soil mixed with ericaceous compost. Plant pot-grown camomile plants about 10 cm apart, in March to May. Once your bed has filled out a bit, just add a couple of pillows. The camomile will release its fragrance every time you use your bed. Keep it well watered in summer and trim with a strimmer.

320

Next time your partner enthuses about something, see if you can plan a break around it. So if he's bopping round the kitchen to the Red Hot Chili Peppers, buy a pair of out-of-town tickets and make a surprise weekend of it.

321

It's easy to have a harmonious relationship when the sky is blue, the sun is shining and you're basking on a golden beach. Ever thought that feeling ought to be bottled? Well, hey, it has. Give each other a massage with last year's sun tan lotion and transport yourselves from Harlow back to Hawaii.

322

For a welcoming and cosy boudoir swap those bright 100-watt bulbs for mellower, warmer 40- or 60-watt versions. And keep a supply of scented tealights on hand for when you're entertaining…

323

One evening sit down and reminisce. Go through your first date, what you wore, what you did. Talk about all the things that first attracted you to each other. Was it the way he talked, something he said? Was it a certain skirt she wore, the way she flicked her hair? This should bring back happy memories and rekindle lustful thoughts.

324

Look for easy ways to cheer your partner up. Pick up a tub of her favourite ice-cream on the way home from work. Run him a bath and bring him a beer. Sappy gestures work – they build up a huge bank of goodwill that couples can draw on when life gets stressful.

325

Kissing and embracing is a vital part of any lover's repertoire. Start today and make kissing part of your daily routine. Practice kissing hello and goodbye, and take it from there.

326

If you're having a seductive dinner with your loved one, try something classical. It's wise to steer clear of opera as it can get a bit screechy and spoil an intimate moment. Try soul for raunchy sex and Brazilian samba when you want to get really hot and passionate. Something mellow and atmospheric works well for the aperitif: just make sure it's not going to make you sleepy.

327

Try a sensual aromatherapy massage to get you both in a loving mood. Just add five drops of your chosen essential oil to 20 ml of a carrier oil, such as almond or sunflower. Lavender, rose and camomile are all good relaxers.

328

Take turns to 'spoon' each other, lying side by side. Synchronise your breathing so you are inhaling and exhaling at the same time. This has an almost magical effect in bringing you closer to each other and getting you back on each other's wavelength.

329

Next time you go watch a film that moves you and brings you closer, buy your partner the soundtrack. Listening to it will bring back strong feelings and help you hold on to the intimacy.

330

Next time you see your partner, touch before speaking. If he's in the kitchen washing up, sneak up behind him, slide your hands round his tummy and cuddle up. When she comes home from work, give her a long hug instead of firing questions or filing complaints.

331

Do activities together with your partner that you both enjoy so you keep your relationship sparking and alive. Go to the gym together, go to the cinema and sit on the back row so you can snog and hold hands, or share something exciting like your first trip in a hot air balloon.

332

When you can't make a whole evening of it, you can at least go to bed early and lock the door. Make your bedroom as sensuous as possible. It's really worth investing in Egyptian cotton sheets, duvet covers and pillow cases – they feel great and get softer the more you wash them. Strew rose petals on the bed, light the room with scented candles, draw the curtains and relax. Don't forget to take the phone off the hook.

be arsed...
to do something that scares you

(if you've always wanted to but never dared – seize the moment)

11

333

Want to change a limiting belief into an empowering one? Rewire the negative neural track created in the brain. You do this in exactly the same way the track was created: by using self-talk or affirmations. An affirmation is a positive statement of fact or belief in the present tense that will lead you towards the end result you expect (e.g. 'I am strong and confident'). As you 're-programme', repeat it aloud every day for between 5 and 20 minutes.

334

When skiing, the more time you spend on steep slopes, the less scary they will seem. Even if you're not ready to carve up on the back bowls yet, get yourself on those steep slopes and simply sideslip your way down. Just reaching the bottom, no matter how unstylishly, will make the slope seem less daunting next time.

335

Find some large bin-liners. Open your wardrobe. Take out any clothes that you haven't worn for over a year, or that you've no realistic chance (be honest here) of fitting into again, and put these into the bags. Drive straightaway to your nearest charity shop and hand everything over. Leave without looking back. You will feel better, without a doubt.

336

Try hang gliding. To get an idea of whether it is for you it is not necessary to put yourself through a ten-day course. There are taster courses which give you a basic introduction and have you performing short skims (as far as I'm concerned when your feet are off the ground you're flying) in a day or so. Better yet, sign up for a tandem flight where you will be in a sling alongside the instructor so you not only get to fly but can listen to the explanations of how to control the wing, without the responsibility of flying/crashing it yourself.

337

Too nervous for daredevil sports? Book a lesson in a controlled environment, with an instructor watching your every move and lots of first class equipment. There may not be a tame version of a bungee jump, but what about learning to ski on a dry ski slope, or practising scuba diving in the local pool?

338

If you've got a wedding speech now inked firmly in your diary, start immediately to prepare it. Just dump down ideas (memories, stories, things you think you might be able to use from elsewhere, anecdotes that have made you laugh, etc.). Don't worry about having too much material and too little shape. A couple of weeks before the event, start to knead it and shape it into two or three stories. Pinch bits from here and bits from there to embellish them – and pretty soon you will have all you need.

339

Try combining horse trekking and water. There is nothing more satisfying than riding on a beach and urging the horse into the water. Or crossing rivers. Apart from an oddly at-one-with-nature feeling about riding above the waters on a large animal it is a great way to see wildlife.

340

Feeling the fear? Women seem to experience fear more often and more intensely than men. Don't let inappropriate fear paralyse you. Instead, when you feel scared, take five long, deep breaths and repeat to yourself all the reasons why your fear is irrational.

Give your latest leisure activity more spice by setting yourself a challenge. If you're doing something energetic, like running or swimming, choose a suitable target distance and aim to raise some cash for charity by getting sponsored. If you're learning to jive, enter the first of next year's competitive events. You can't find a challenge? There's always a way of gingering up even a mundane activity.

Face your finances. When the statements for your cards turn up over the next few weeks, make a note of the interest charged in each case, tot up the total interest you pay each month and multiply it by 12. That will give you a ballpark figure for the year. If that doesn't make you cry out in anguish, you may be beyond redemption.

343

Want to learn about getting airborne without paying for it? Every hot air balloon launch requires a couple of crew to help rig up the craft, hold the balloon while it is being filled with hot air, then follow it on the ground and help pack it up again. It's spear-carrying stuff and very few flight schools pay their crew but on the other hand they usually will thank you with balloon rides or flying lessons. If you have a little free time then crewing is the ideal way to find out if ballooning is for you.

344

Go commando. Going out without wearing your underwear makes you feel amazingly sexy. And it's a secret only you know, until you decide to share it with your partner of course…

345

Is there something holding you back from achieving something you've always wanted to achieve? Perhaps there's a subconscious belief that's stopping you. See if you can find it by asking yourself what you're assuming about this situation. Write down whatever responses come into your mind, however crazy they might seem. You may then choose to ask yourself a question along the lines of, 'If I could change my life to be exactly as I want it to be, what would I do differently, right now?'

346

Heli skiing is a great thrill but it hurts. Right in the wallet. So how about a halfway house that gets you off the beaten track but doesn't take a second mortgage to finance? That's the idea behind 'cat' skiing. The cat in question is a snowcat: a tracked vehicle that trundles up the snow faces to take you away from it all and then back down to pick you up ready for another go. Snowcats offer one of the cheapest ways of getting out onto virgin powder, travel far and wide to find snow, are never grounded by mist and would be hard pushed to tumble out of the sky.

347

Become a lap dancer in the privacy of your own home. It's easy to learn how. Have a search for online tips or rent movies featuring stripping such as *Striptease* and *Showgirls*. It's fairly straightforward though: just dance seductively wearing very little while your partner/audience stuffs cash into your g-string; sexy, fun and profitable. Some exercise classes now use pole dancing as a way to fitness. Check out Polestars, which has a great website.

348

If you want to play the markets, why not try a spread bet or an exchange bet on the values of the FTSE, or of currency? All the spread betting firms offer financial bets, because most of their customers work in the City. And Betfair has introduced a range of financial bets which combine the feel and language of a sports bet with the volatility and unpredictability of the stock market.

349

Tired of traditional bungee, you globe-trotting daredevil, you? OK, then try reverse bungee. In reverse bungee you are strapped into a pod (usually two of you at once) which is suspended between two towers and connected to them both by enormous elastic. If you ever played with a catapult/slingshot when you were a kid then you can probably guess what comes next. The elastic takes up the slack, the pod is released and you go flying off into the sky. Most operators have a small video camera attached to the pod filming your reaction so when your stomach has returned to normal you can have a giggle at your zero-g gurning.

350

Is there something that makes you a little anxious or very scared, in a business setting? Presentations come to mind for many, of course. Perhaps tackling difficult people or chasing for late payments or… you've got a few; everyone has. Whatever it is, do it, tackle that fear, because once you have you will feel so good. That presentation, or picking up the phone and chasing that person who has been holding back your overdue payment – do it now.

351

If you lack confidence, commit yourself to some kind of group action. Choose your activity, pay in advance, get it in your diary, and arrange to meet someone there. For example, if you're not as fit as you'd like to be, join a local exercise class. If there isn't one around, have a word with your local health club and get one started. If you've retreated into your shell, pick up the phone and book up for a series of classes in something you've never tried before – local colleges run everything from am-dram to woodwork.

352

Try a taster triathlon. Often called a 'Try a Tri' or a 'Super Sprint' these events are held by clubs to encourage newcomers and often involve distances along the lines of a 200 m swim, a 10 km cycle and a 2 or 3 km run. If, like most people, it's the swim leg that worries you most then make sure that it is held in a swimming pool rather than open water. That way not only is it less threatening but you can also stand up any time you get tired. If you feel the splish is really getting on top of you then you can even walk the water stretch, if that's what works for you.

353

Swap your home with someone from another country for a few weeks. House-swap companies can arrange it for you, or maybe you already know someone living overseas who'd love the chance to come back and see old friends from the comfort of your home, while you enjoy theirs?

354

Think of a situation that you currently avoid as it makes you nervous, such as speaking your mind in front of colleagues or your boss, joining a club to meet new people or going to a party where you don't know anybody. Completely let go of how you feel about yourself and think about what you can give to others in this situation, such as giving your colleagues the courage to open up themselves, giving your boss a chance to understand you better or meeting a shy person at the party and showing them care and support. Promise yourself that you'll do one thing each week, however small, where previously you held back through lack of confidence and see how differently you begin to feel.

355

If you have to give a speech an audio recorder is a useful aid – it helps to get the timing right for each section. A few replays will help you to remember the contents triggered by your key words or phrases.

356

Take any daily habit. Your route to work, the time you get up. The cereal you eat, the time you check your e-mail. Break it! Take a different route to work. Eat a different cereal… It's fun isn't it? Break a few more! It's small stuff, agreed. But, by doing this, you have just got better at breaking patterns.

357

Try caving. There are commercial caves out there offering guided tours of grottoes or the entrances to systems but for a real taste of caving your best bet is to contact a local club (universities are often a good bet if you're having trouble finding one). Caving clubs are usually delighted to take newbies on a trip to their favourite sites and will be able to lend or rent you all the kit you need so you don't have to buy anything unless you're sure you will get good use out of it. Going the club route (or 'grottoes' as they're called in the States) means you get easy access to expertise, logistics and general organisation and can come back bragging merrily about not just getting off the beaten track but burrowing far beneath it.

358

Enjoy abseiling and want to try something a little more challenging? Easy. Turn over. Rap jumping was developed by the military as a means of abseiling out of helicopters, etc., while still being able to point and shoot at the bad guys below. For rap jumping the carabiner is clipped to the back of your harness and you just use one hand in front of you to feed the rope; the other one holds the Uzi/cigarette holder/champagne glass (depending on your personal style). At the top you lower 'into' the rope facing down so you are at right angles to the cliff, and then you start to 'run' down the face.

The faster you can feed rope the easier it is to run or jump and oddly enough this makes the process much more stable than taking it slowly and trying to place your feet as you go. Not for the faint-hearted but tons of fun.

359

Take up life drawing. Not only will you get to see men and women pose naked but you will acquire a talent and meet new people. All of whom like naked bodies. There are life drawing classes all over the place, contact your local council for more information or look online.

360

If you have to end a relationship, don't set the whole dumping thing up over time by saying 'We need to talk', 'Let's get together some time and see where we stand', that sort of thing. This isn't going to help get the whole thing done without recrimination. Always remember, speed and efficiency are best for both of you. Surgeons don't remove an appendix by spending two weeks prodding the area with a scalpel to see what happens.

361

What about extreme ironing? Some of the great achievements remain tantalisingly out of reach; for example, while Base Camp has been ironed, no ironist to date has been photographed chasing out the crumples at the summit of Everest. Somewhere out there is a budding ironist just waiting to scale that pinnacle of human achievement. See if there are any gaps that have yet to be ironed - it might be ironing in a particular location, or it might be that nobody has yet combined the purity of extreme ironing with your own preferred adventure sport (heli bungee ironing, anyone?).

The opportunities are legion, and the chance to become a legend in laundry is there for the taking.

363

Downshift for a better quality of life. Dare to daydream. Create the picture of how you want your downshifted life to be. Once you have this in your mind, craft your list of pros – more time with the children, less stress, no commuting, being more self-sufficient. But consider the cons too. Will you be able to cope with isolation, hard work, harsh weather and surviving on a reduced income? Read as many personal accounts of downshifting as possible so you get a realistic picture of the bliss – and agony – you may experience.

362

Have some fun and get some confidence by taking self-defence classes. Lots of organisations run them and, if you're female and nervous about going to a mixed class, some of them are run for women only.

364

Create an action plan. All too often we talk about wanting to get fitter, visit friends or take up a new hobby, but another year passes and we never seem to get around to it. Head up columns with the areas you wish to work on, then create two rows for listing exactly how you intend to go about the change and when you intend to achieve this by. Also include a 'completed' box. The key is to break the path to success down into small, realistic and achievable steps.

365

Try paragliding. Tandem flights are the best way to go for beginners because you can find out whether or not you like it without spending time learning about aerodynamics and meteorology. Even intermediates can still learn a lot from a tandem flight as it's the best chance you'll get to observe the experts from close up. They couldn't be simpler. Your pilot will lay out the glider, clip you into the harness and tell you when to run. You leg it, and before you know it your legs are still trying to run but you're not actually touching the ground. From there on you can relax and enjoy the view.